9/11

An Astrological Tribute to September 11

Edited by Louis E.V. Nevaer

9/11: An Astrological Tribute to September 11
Copyright © 2014 by Casa Catherwood, an imprint of Hispanic Economics, Inc. Manufactured in the United States of America. All rights reserved. No part of this book may be reproduced in any form or by any means, electronic or mechanical, including photocopying, recording, or by information storage and retrieval systems—except by a reviewer who may quote brief passages in a review to be printed in a magazine, newspaper or on the Internet—without permission in writing from the publisher.
This book is presented solely for educational and informational purposes.
First printing 2014
Publication date: April 2014.

ATTENTION CORPORATIONS, UNIVERSITIES, COLLEGES, AND PROFESSIONAL AND CHARITABLE ORGANIZATIONS: Quantity discounts are available on bulk purchases of this book for educational and gift purposes, or as premiums in fundraising efforts. Inquiries should be sent to *info@hispaniceconomics.com*.

Casa Catherwood
Calle 59 #572, por 72 & 74
Colonia Centro
Mérida, Yucatán, Mexico
www.casa-catherwood.com
info@casa-catherwood.com

Casa Catherwood is an imprint of Hispanic Economics, Inc.
P.O. Box 140681
Coral Gables, FL 33114-0681
info@hispaniceconomics.com

Royalties from the sale of this book are being donated to the September 11 Memorial and Museum. Readers may send their donations to:
National September 11 Memorial and Museum at the World Trade Center Foundation, Inc.
200 Liberty Street, 16th Floor
New York, NY 10281

ISBN 978-1-939879-12-7

Cover and Interior Design by John Clifton
john@johnclifton.net

Contents

Introduction - 7

911 Victims Arranged by Astrological Sign - 9

Aries - 9

Taurus - 11

Gemini - 13

Cancer - 15

Leo - 17

Virgo - 19

Libra -21

Scorpio - 23

Sagittarius - 25

Capricorn - 27

Aquarius - 29

Pisces - 31

The Flights and Those Aboard - 33

American Airlines Flight 11 - 33

American Airlines Flight 77 - 36

United Airlines Flight 93 - 38

United Airlines Flight 175 - 39

United Airlines Flight 175 - 40

The Buildings The Pentagon - 43

The World Trade Center - 47

The Others - 124

Hijackers - 124

First Responders - 125

The Absent - 128

Islam at the World Trade Center - 129

Support - 130

Donating to the September 11 Memorial and Museum - 130

Editor's Notes - 130

The city, for the first time in its long history, is destructible. A single flight of planes no bigger than a wedge of geese can quickly end this island fantasy, burn the towers, crumble the bridges, turn the underground passages into lethal chambers, cremate the millions. The intimation of mortality is part of New York now; in the sounds of jets overhead, in the black headlines of the latest editions.

—E. B. White, *Here is New York*, 1949

Introduction

If you were living in New York, as I was, during the terrorist attack of September 11, 2001, you remember that in the weeks and months that followed, as smoke still rose from Ground Zero and as the around-the-clock recovery efforts continued, one question occupied most polite conversations.

It centered on a nagging thought, a curiosity, a great unknown. At business meetings, over tea with friends at cafés, and at dinner parties all over town, the conversation often turned to this compelling question: Where did the heroes who perished that morning of unspeakable horror live?

By ZIP code.

Was it 10005, 10013, or 10021?

No one knew and everyone wanted to know.

Enter the *New York Times*.

"Almost from the moment that the World Trade Center towers collapsed on Sept. 11, as people attempted to grasp the magnitude of the attack by tallying losses, they have tried to figure out which towns and neighborhoods were worst hit," Andy Newman reported in the *Times* on August 21, 2002. "Now with the New York City medical examiner office's release on Monday of the most thorough list of victims, it is possible to chart the devastation by ZIP code."

New Yorkers who had waited more than 11 months to find out the definitive answer now knew: "[J]udged another way, by per capita, the highest death rate in a town of considerable size was in Hoboken, N.J., 07030, across the Hudson River from Manhattan."

Not New York?

The report continued: "The ZIP code analysis also shows that while the attack occurred in New York City, most of those who died—more than 55 percent—lived elsewhere, whether they were commuters working downtown or passengers on the two hijacked flights that struck the towers."

New York had been attacked, but New Yorkers were a minority of the victims.

Life is seldom what one expects.

In 2002, *Missing: Last Seen at the World Trade Center* traveled to seventeen cities across the nation and was seen by almost 1.7 million visitors. As curator, I accompanied that exhibition of the missing person flyers, and I recall being taken aback by the number of visitors who came up to me to inquire about astrology and horoscopes. That so many Americans believe in astrology—I could not even recite the twelve astrological signs—surprised me. I had no answer to offer any of them. Indeed, I was unprepared for the mysticism that permeated Americans' struggle to make sense of the events that had transpired on September 11, 2001.

With the opening of the 9/11 Memorial Museum in May 2014, however, it is auspicious that this book, honoring those lost on that fateful day by including astrological information, becomes available to answer the questions many have had these past thirteen years.

Were their destinies in the stars?

Is there cosmic sense that explains why the individuals who died were destined to die that terrible day?

Who can tell?

What is known is that on a beautiful fall day four hijacked commercial airliners destroyed the Twin Towers, struck the Pentagon, and crashed in rural Pennsylvania, killing almost 3,000 people.

The most represented zodiacal sign among those who died was Leo.

The least represented was Sagittarius.

Almost a quarter of those who died at the Pentagon were Libras or Aries.

Thirty percent of those aboard the four hijacked planes were Libras, Virgos, or Geminis.

There were more Leos than any other sign among the hijackers.

What if I told you Leo is a Fire sign associated with zealotry?

What are the chances that, among the victims, the only two men named Rocco shared the same birthday? Or that three of the innocents slain were named Michael Lynch?

Do any of these facts mean anything? Can one surmise patterns—or infer a cosmic purpose?

In 1927, Thorton Wilder published a novel, *The Bridge of San Luis Rey*, that tells the story of the individuals who perished in the collapse of a rope bridge in the Andes mountain ranges of Peru. In that narrative, Brother Juniper, a Franciscan monk, embarks on a quest to find a cosmic answer to the question why those specific individuals died that day when the bridge collapsed. Hundreds of people crossed the bridge every day.

Why were these individuals crossing the bridge at the exact moment when the bridge collapsed?

The philosophical questions Wilder asks in his work of fiction are the same ones contemplated with anguish almost three quarters of a century later.

Why did those specific passengers and crewmembers board those specific planes?

Why were those 125 individuals at the Pentagon in those specific offices that morning?

Why were the individuals at the World Trade Center there on that Tuesday—and not anywhere else?

Why were so many first responders trapped at the site that would henceforth be known as Ground Zero?

Was it in the stars?

In *The Bridge of San Luis Rey*, Wilder concludes that "there is a land of the living and a land of the dead and the bridge is love, the only survival, the only meaning."

Perhaps the same can be said of the events of September 11, 2001.

Louis E.V. Nevaer
New York, NY

9/11 Victims Arranged by Astrological Sign

Aries

March 21
Brian
Deborah
Edmund
Harry
Jesús
Judith
Raymond
Thomas

March 22
Adriana
Andrew
Dianne
Gregg
Joseph
Michael
Stacey

March 23
Carrie
Courtney
Dianne
James
José
Robert
Scott
Stephen
Victoria
Vito
William

March 24
David
Eduvigis
Gerard
Gregory
Joseph
Matthew
Michael
Mildred
Paul
Richard
Robert

March 25
Babita
Daniel
Debbie
Dino
Elizabeth
Gavin

March 26
Andrew
Bella
Christine
Edward
Michael
Michael H.
Richard
Takashi

March 27
Carolyn
Janice
John
Joseph
Keiji
Mark
Marni
Michael
Michelle
Raymond

March 28
Frances
Gerald
Jane
Jean
Joseph
Simon
Stanley

March 29
Donna
James
Jeffrey
Kirsten
Mary
Steve
Thomas

March 30
Anne
Dean
Dong
Franklin
Joseph
Maria
Patrick
Sheila
Stephen

March 31
Allan
Anthony
Brian
Chantal
Francis
Hilda

Jeffrey
Joseph
Joseph A.
Lance
Mark
Paul
Robert
Robert D.
Yugi

April 1
Ana
Dennis
Ludwig
Marcia
Nickie
Oscar
Robert
Salvatore
Victor
Yin

April 2
Douglas
Francisco
James
Jerrold
Michael

April 3
Frederick
John
Kathleen
Robert
Virginia

April 4
Brady
Jeffrey
Mauricio
Muriel
Sara
Thomas

April 5
Andre
Barbara
Jeffrey
Joseph
Joseph V.
Mark

April 6
Christopher
David
David T.
Edward
Garth
Michael
Michael J.
Peter
Ramón
Rosa
Stanley

April 7
Eugene
Scott

April 8
David
David W.

Deora
Keiichiro
Lindsay
Molly
Oliver
Ralph
Roberta

April 9
Brandon
Erica
Robert
Stephen
William

April 10
Alison
David
Efrain
George
Joseph
Ricardo
Steven

April 11
Alex
Atsushi
Carlos
Edward
John
Joseph
Lyudmila
Paul
Susan

April 12
Jennifer
Niurka
Vincent

April 13
Bernard
Joseph
Steven

April 14
Berinthia
Joshua
Michael
Michael A.
Phyllis
Satoshi
Stanley
Steven

April 15
Ann
Edward
Faustino
Hernando
John
Juan
Kathryn
Kenneth
Susan
Tamara
Vincent

April 16
Gerard
Jack

John
Keith
Kevin
Martin
Matthew
Ruth

April 17
Alfonse
Andrew
Eric
Jayesh
Steven
Thomas
Thomas A.

April 18
Abigail
Alva
Liam
Paul
Stephen
William
William E.

April 19
Edna
Edward
Edward V.
Eric
Fitzroy
Glenn
Jeffrey
Mary
Myrna
Natalie

Taurus

April 20
Andrew
Daniel
David
Gregory
John
Jonathan
Julian
Peter
Robert
Sharon
Thomas

April 21
Adriane
Arlene
Cira
Karol
Khamladai
Linda
Marcia
Nizam
Peter

April 22
Alan
Boris
Brigette
Charles
Cheryle
Debbie
Jack
Jessica
Robert

April 23
Alan
Daniela
Gayle
Jorge
Norma
Peter
Sebastian

April 24
Abraham
Alexander
Christopher
Georgine
Jon
Renee
Samuel
Susan
Thomas

April 25
Aleksandr
Carl
Jerome
Joanne
Kevin
Patricia
Peter
Prokopios
Wayne
William

April 26
Dennis
Donald
Edward
Joseph
Linda
Michele
Michelle
Richard
Robert
Vinod
Yuk

April 27
Andrew
Charles
Dennis
Richard
Robert
Robert W.
Rosanne
Rosemary
Sanae
Thomas

April 28
Claudia
David
Dennis
Edward
John
Marion
Rudolph

April 29
Jennifer
Joanne
Maclovio
Matthew
Neil
Robert
William

April 30
Cesar
Charles
Jason
Joshua
Leanne
Marian
Marion
Richard
Ronald
Ryan
Wai-Ching

May 1
Angel
David
Diane
Japhet
Norma
Shai
Tariq
Wei

May 2
Avnish
Carl
Cono
Cora
Lincoln
Peter
Sheila

May 3
Abdu
Alok
Barbara
Donald
Edward
Francis
Harvey
Khalid
Laura
Mark
Ronald
Tara

May 4
Daniel
Juliana
Matthew
Patricia
Peter
Stephen
William

May 5
Arthur
Christopher
Evan
Glenn
H. Joseph
James
Seamus

May 6
Daniel
Deepika
Dennis
Dolores
Edward
Harvey
Howard
Joseph
Joseph R.
Marlyn
Michael
Raymond
Robert
Ronald

May 7
Arthur
Carol
Robert
Rubén

May 8
Brian
Christopher
Christopher M.
James
Jeremy
Judy
Paul

May 9
Brian
Fanny
Ivan
James
Mark
Stephen
Susan
Susan L.
Timothy
Vladimir
Hijacker

May 10
Alexander
Gricelda
James
Lisa
Perry

May 11
Andre
Anthony
David
Edward
Jill
Krishna
Lucille
Mychal
Robert
Robert
Santos
Thomas
Hijacker

May 12
Antonio
Gary
Kaaria
Mark
Philip
Suzanne
Terence

May 13
Fabian
George
James
Kathy
Kenneth
Kenneth J.
Renee
Samuel
William

May 14
Daniel
Edward
Jeff
Michael
Michael P.
Michael T.
Takashi
William

May 15
Daniel
Isidro
John
Orasri
Robin
Ronald
Thomas
Vassilios
William

May 16
Brock
Charles
Debora
Jennifer
Mannie
Maria
Samantha
Hijacker

May 17
Ann
Barrington
David
Jon
Joseph
Richard
Richard L.
Robert
Stanley
Welles

May 18
Eddie
Eugene
Michael
Michael S.
Richard
Thomas
Todd

May 19
Eric
John
Louie
Manette
Marco
Peter
Stephen
Wilbert

May 20
Eustace
Gabriela
Jacqueline
Jean
John
Joseph
Kyung
Michael

Gemini

May 21
Brian
Daniel
Donald
Jie
John
Lourdes
Paul
Steve
Tatyana
Vincent

May 22
Edmond
Elena
Ivan
Kristin
Mark
Walter

May 23
Aaron
Corey
David
Dennis
Goumatie
James
Richard
Veronique
Vincent

May 24
Andrea
Dean
James
Jim
John
Joseph
Sean
Sean T.
Susan

May 25
Ferdinand
Jack
John
John C.
John S.
Manuel
Michael
Michelle
Steven

May 26
Angel
Calvin
Derek
Gerald
Jeffrey
John
Kazuhiro
Marsha
Nicholas
Robert

May 27
Bernard
Christian
Karen
Lucia
Lynn
Matthew
Michael
Paul
Randolph
Richard
Scott

May 28
Denease
Edward
Gerald
Ming
Neil
Paul
Thomas
Valsa
Hijacker

May 29
Albert
Damian
Lawrence
Louis
Melissa
Thomas

May 30
Donald
Karlie
Lesley
Michael
Robert

May 31
Amy
Anthony
David S.
Joseph
Maria
Robert

June 1
Barbara
Christopher
Darryl
Dorota
Janice
Jeffrey
Paul
Steve

June 2
Antonio

CeCelia
Donna
Douglas
Douglas F.
Jane
Jill
John
Nurul
Robert
Vivian

June 3
Bradley
Davin
Joseph
Louise
Mohammed
Richard
Scott
Scott T.
Swede

June 4
Anthony
Colleen
David
Francis
Glenn
James
Joshua
Lynette

Ruth
Thomas

June 5
Alan
Jason
John
Kenneth
Lorraine
Robert
Thomas

June 6
Allen
Aram
David
Dora
Ralph
Robert

June 7
Alisha
Brian
Francine
Gary
John
Luis
Michael
Michael Edward
Paige
Patrick
Scott
Steven

June 8
John
Leonard
Lonny
Richard
Thomas

June 9
Adam
Christopher
Ginger

Glen
Godwin
Jay
John
Joseph
Joseph A.
Karen
Kathryn
Marsha
Stephen
Stephen P.

June 10
Alejo
Anthony
Christopher
David
Edward
Joanne
Lamar
Linda
Maria
Nina
Robert
Sandra
Touri

June 11
Alicia
Brian
Daniel
Daniel H.
David
Dennis
Farah
Iouri
Joseph
Linda
Mark
Robert
Robert L.

June 12
Anthony
Jane

Joseph
Heather
Karl
Keith
Steven

June 13
Alvin
Anthony
Antonio
David
Digna
Eric
Garnet
James
John
Lisa
Michael
Sandra

June 14
Brian
Emelda
Mary
Robert
Robert E.
SeiLai
Weibin

June 15
Christopher
Donnie
John A.
Katherine
Michael
Pendyala
Peter
Rafael
Rita

June 16
Alena
Leobardo
Virginia

June 17
Joshua
Joyce

June 18
Dominick
Franco
James
Richard
Ricknauth
Sean
William
Hijacker

June 19
Anna
Bernard
Brian
Betsy
Calixto
Malissa
Mari-Rae
Mark
Martha
Sandra

June 20
Ada
Amy
Christine
Felicia
Harvey
Howard
Jesús
Martin
Matthew
Michael
Michael J.
Scott
Thomas

Cancer

June 21
Alona
Jeff
Johanna

June 22
Christopher
Daniel
James
Michael
William
Ye Wei

June 23
Carol
David
Douglas
Gary
George
Matthew
Robert

June 24
Beverly
Colin
Jan
John
Louis
Tonyell

June 25
Arthur
Igor
Josh
Lisa
Luke
Meredith
Patrick
Patrick M.

June 26
Inna
James
Jeffrey
John
Kathleen
Kevin
Paul
Scott
Sonia
Stewart

June 27
Andrew
Ernest
Joseph
Juan
Kenneth
Michele

June 28
Carl
Christopher
Cindy
Don
Jean
Shawn
Yelena
Hijacker

June 29
Arcangel
Joshua
Robert
Yvonne

June 30
Benjamin
Jacqueline
John
John G.
Richard
Robert
Ron
Simon
Todd

July 1
Alysia
Carrie
Dennis
Edward
Marcello
Martin
Richard
Thomas
Tu-Anh

July 2
Aisha
Alan
Charles
Clifford
David
Deborah
Ivelin
Jeffrey
Kevin
Nicholas
Nicholas P.
Richard
Robert
William
Hijacker

July 3
Ching
Donald
Edward
Eli
Helen
Sara

July 4
Christine
Daniel
Daniel J.
James
John
John Philip
Kenneth
Richard
Sergio
Stephen
Valerie

July 5
Clive
Edwin
Frederick
Giovanna
Ingeborg
John
Leonel
Timothy

July 6
Douglas
Frank
Joseph
Kristen
Manuel
Michael

July 7
Alexander
Anthony
Bruce
Hector
Herman
Jennifer
Michael
Shawn

July 8
Christopher
Danielle
Florence
Thomas

July 9
Charles
Charles A.
Kenneth
Michele

July 10
Charles
Donald
Glenn
James
Kevin
Mario
Richard
Robert

July 11
Colin
Douglas
Edward
Kevin
Leon
Michael
Paul
Odessa

July 12
Azael
Charles
James
Jason
Kenneth
Richard
Victor

July 13
Ana
Anthony
Donald
Kevin
Michael

July 14
Bernard
Diane
Joanne
Leon

Mark
Stephen
William

July 15
Bernard
Enrique
John
Jonathan
Michael
Michael L.
Paul
Timothy
Vanavah

July 16
Alexis
Alfred
George
John
John R.
Michelle
Raymond
Wendy

July 17
Barbara
Eddie
Jeffrey
Kenneth
Michele
Patrick
Paul
Simon

July 18
Judson
Louis
Todd

July 19
Jeanette
Kris
Patrick
Thomas

July 20
Brent
Brian
Deborah
Lorraine
Lydia
Mark
Michael
Muhammadou
Robert
Robert M.
Stephen
William
William T.
Yelena

July 21
Charles
Dana
David M.
Edward
James
James R.
Joseph
Luis
Patricia
Sean
Shimmy

July 22
Edward
Eric
James
James L.
James P.
Linda
Mary
Nancy
Patrick
Steven
Walter

Leo

July 23
Adam
Alan
Allison
Diane
Eileen
Felix
James
John
John T.
Michael
Ronnie
Steven
Thomas

July 24
Alex
Gavkharoy
James
Judith
Max
Patrick
Paul

July 25
R. Bruce
Carlton
Daphne
David
Jackie
Richard
Ronald
Scott

Stephanie
Steven
Wendy

July 26
Danny
Felicia
Frederick
Garo
Heinrich
James
JoAnn
Kevin
Kevin P.
Michael
Sarah
Sean
Suzanne
Ulf

July 27
Gino
John
Michael
Robert
Sheldon
William

July 28
Christopher
Douglas
James

John
Krystine
Monica
Naomi
Sue Kim

July 29
Bryan
Colleen
Harry
Jake
James
Jerry
Ralph
Yvette

July 30
Angela
Anil
Brandon
Gregg
Jerry
Leonard
Michael
Michael P.
Paul
Salvatore
William

July 31
Anthony
Ayleen
Bruce

Catherine
Charles
Dennis
Eileen
John
John G.
Matthew
Paul
Raphael
Robert
Stuart
Vincent
Hijacker

August 1
Angelo
Deanna
Frederick
Heather
Jimmie
Joseph
Richard
Thomas

August 2
Benjamin
David
Erik
Grace
Howard

James
Jeannine
John
Karamo
Michael
Thomas
William

August 3
Geoffrey
José
Joseph
Joseph J.
Matthew

August 4
Anthony
David
Joseph
Kevin
Loretta
Ronald
Vincent
Walter

August 5
Ernest
Samuel
Sanford

August 6
Gary
Harry
Nancy
Peter
Roshan
Wendy
William

August 7
Anthony
Anthony R.

Erwin
Frank
Jeanmarie
Mark
Sandra
Tyler

August 8
Christopher
Christopher S.
Dorothy
Elizabeth
Gordon
Michael
Michelle
Patrice
Ronnie
Samuel

August 9
Adianes
Carl
Cynthia
Meredith
Monica
Robert
Sonia
Thomas
Hijacker

August 10
Brian
Christina
Craig
Leo
Nancy
Peter
Philip
Rebecca
Timothy

August 11
David
Diana
Laura
Mary
Ronald
Takashi

August 12
Anne
Christine
Frank
Gilbert
Joan
Joseph
Paul
Ryan
William

August 13
Bruce
Christopher
Darya
Diane
Jason
Norma
Paul
Robert
Shabbir
Takuya
Hijacker

August 14
Janet
Julie
Matthew
Richard
Scott
Thomas

August 15
Dominick

Keith
Margaret
Maria
Paul
Peter
Stephen
Stephen J.
Tara

August 16
Alok
Joseph
Margaret
Margaret L.

August 17
Alexey
Deepa
Gerald
Leonard
Louis
Martin
Neil
Robert
Roko
Ronald
Saranya
William
Yoichi
Hijacker
Hijacker

August 18
Dorothy
Howard
Jon Charles
Joseph

August 19
Alan
Daniel
Diarelia

Durrell
Elsy
Kevin
Luis
Neil
Peter
Robert
Robert J.
Ramzi
Sol
Steven
Timothy

August 20
Andrew
Brian
Christopher
Francisco
Kevin
Leonard
Mark
Patricia
Shakila

August 21
Benjamin
Craig
Daniel
Teresa
Thomas

August 22
Carmen
Douglas
James
Linda
Mary
Uhuru
Wanda

Virgo

August 23
Bettina
Francis
Kevin
Nestor

August 24
Catherine
Christopher
Colleen
Darin
David
Frank
Michael
Montgomery
Sarah

August 25
Andrew
Christian
Craig
Keith
Masaru
Patricia
Waleed

August 26
Alvin
Charles
Gary
John
Kevin
Kristen
Michael
Peter
Richard
Robert
Sherry
Stacey
Tamitha

August 27
Donald
Jenny
José
Leroy
Lindsay
Margaret
Peter Edward
Peter Mark
Suria

August 28
Brooke
Edward
Maria
Seima

August 29
Andrew
David
Elizabeth
Francis
Gregory
Kiran
Laura
Olga
Rayman
Terence
Victor
Yudhvir

August 30
Doris
Dorothy
Jesús
Kenneth
Palmina
Ronald
Suresh
Tarel
Thomas

August 31
Carl
Catherine
James
John
John T.
Lauren
Michael
Philip
Robert
Steven
Wesley
William

September 1
Blanca
Edward
Giovanna
Ian
Kevin
Melissa
Prem
Thomas
Hijacker

September 2
Everett
Kathleen
Larry
Mark
Michael
Michael J.
Norbert
Paul
Thomas

September 3
Barry
Jeffrey
Jeremy
Timothy

September 4
Adele
James
John
Jonathan
Jorge
Kristine

Liming
Obdulio
Paul
Stacey
Susan
Tawanna

September 5
Dipti
Esmerlin
George
Joanne
John
Kip
Terence
Timothy
William

September 6
Andrew
Angela
Brian
Claribel
Elaine
Eugenia
John
Kenneth
Kevin
Michael
Valerie

September 7
Gertrude
Vaswald

September 8
Alexandru
David
Jeremiah
Joseph
Michael

Michael D.
Michael P.
Steven
Thomas

September 9
Carlton
Jody
Louis
Philip
Robert
Sean

September 10
David
Pamela

September 11
Amelia
Ann
Ivhan
Michael
Michael P.
Vincent

September 12
Charles
Jimmy
Leah

September 13
Alan
Chin
Dolores
Edelmiro
George
James
John
Linda
Mark
Neal

Nolbert
Ronald
Steven

September 14
Christopher
Kris
Paul
Selina
Thomas

September 15
Christopher
Delrose
Donald
Edward
Glenroy
Harry
Laurence
Mary
Mohammed
Valerie

September 16
Harry
Jenine
Michael
Neil
Shawn

September 17
Ariel
Joel
John
John M.
Suzanne
Vincent

September 18
Charles
Francisco

Jeffrey
Margaret
Michael
Rajesh
Sandra
Steven
Thomas
Vita

September 19
Christopher
Hilario
Justin
Mary
Michael
Pete
Raymond

September 20
Christopher
John
Scott
William

September 21
Abner
Brian
Denise
Donald
Gloria
Patrice
Shari

September 22
Christopher
Craig
Michael
Michael M.
Nicholas
Susan
Wilder

Libra

September 23
Christopher
Frankie
George
Gregory
Peter
Scott
Stephen

September 24
Carole
Carlos
Christy
Donald
Gary
Horace
James
Karl
Kenneth
Raymond
Sankara

September 25
Astrid
Beth
Edward
Evan
Francis
Frank
Gregg
Juan
Lizie
Nancy
Stephen

September 26
Adam
Danielle
Hideya
Martin
Michael
Nicholas
Richard
Robert
Rodney
Terence
Thomas

September 27
Charles
David
James
James K.
Lorraine
Maurice
Noell
Sean
Sylvia

September 28
Chapelle
Earl
Eric Brian
Francisco
Jeffrey
Patrick
Timothy
Victor

September 29
Benilda
Carlos
Darren
Edward
John
John M.
Jonathan
Joseph
Kalyan
Mary
Otis
Paul
Steven
William

September 30
Anna
Douglas
Edward
Godwin
Jorge
Lisa
Maria
Matthew
Patricia
Zhe

October 1
Barry
Jean
Joyce
Lee
Lisa
Michael
Mon
Peter
Stephen
Wayne

October 2
Denis
John J.
Nathaniel
Robert
Walter
Winston

October 3
Allen
Amy
Frederick
Kathleen
Manika
Paul James

October 4
Alayne
Carl
Christopher
Derrick
Dorothy
Frank
Judith
Laura
Oleh
Timothy
Yvette

October 5
Douglas
Gregory
José
Martin
Michael
Robert
Timothy
Zhanetta

October 6
Ana
Billy
Christopher
Edmund
Emerita
Frank
Juanita
Maxima
Milton
Ronald

October 7
James
Jeannine
Kevin Wayne
Marjorie
Mary
Nancy
Peter
William

October 8
Anthony
Boyd
Chandler
Deborah
Diana
Gye
Honor
Juan
Justin
Kevin
Robert
Sandra
Thomas

October 9
Christopher
Gary
Jude
Laurence
Michael
Soichi
Wallace

October 10
Benjamin
Carl
Frank
James
Joseph
Louis
Nichola
Paul
Ramón
Ronald
Vernon

October 11
Edward
Michael
Richard
Stuart
Hijacker

October 12
Christian
David
Gregg
Janice
Joseph
Kenneth
Marie
Maureen
Raul
Roland

October 13
Angel
Glen
James
Jennifer
Laura

October 14
Edna
Elisa
John
Joseph
Michael
Ralph
Shekhar
Taizo

October 15
Alan
Bart
Christopher
Elizabeth
Eric
Manish
Patricia
Ruben
Stephen
Vanessa
Waleska
William
William J.

October 16
Anthony
Elizabeth
Frank
Ingeborg
Jennifer
Robert
Robert A.
William

October 17
Carol
David
Elkin
Eric
Jane
Jon
Michael
Robert

Seth

October 18
Charles
Christian
Cynthia
Gregory
Henry
Janice
Jacquelyn
Peter
Rhonda
Thomas

October 19
Brett
Christopher
Daniel
David
David W.
Denis
Denise
Philip

October 20
Amy
Francesco
Keith
Vernon

October 21
Barbara
Darlene
John
Johnnie
Susan
Toshihiro
Yamel

October 22
Arcelia
Arthur
Catherina
Martin
Paul
Santos

Scorpio

October 23
Anthony
Brian
Ernest
Jacquelyn
José
Lloyd
Robert
Robert C.
Robert W.
Stephen
Tara
Zuhtu

October 24
Hagay
John
Jude
Matthew
Melissa
Michael
Paul
Thomas

October 25
Kenichiro
Lorraine
Mary Jo
Michael
Steven
Vincent

October 26
Robert
Wilson

October 27
Brendan
Charles
Craig
Daniel
James
Jeffrey
John
Judith
Linda
Peter
Sara
Susan
Virginia

October 28
Arlene
Brian
Chih
Christine
Irina
Keith
Laurence
Robert
Steven

October 29
Doreen
Joni
Lawrence
Sigrid

October 30
Brian
David
Jennifer
Klaus
Robert
Vijayashanker
William

October 31
Carl
Christopher
Donna
Edward
Elaine
Matthew
Robert
Ruth Ellen
Stuart
Vanessa

November 1
Dennis
Edward
Jason
Jonas
Shevonne
Ssu-Hui
Wolfgang

November 2
Angela
Jason
Karen
Michael
Nereida
Nestor
Susan

November 3
Andrew
Angel
Conrod
Gary
Glenn
Jean
Joanna
Judith
Karen
Leslie
Terence

November 4
Albert
Charles
Clarin
Craig
Donald
George
Heinrich

Jerome
Joseph
Jupiter
Noel
Sulemanali

November 5
Edgar
Emilio
Gary
Karl
Peter
Peter M.
Robert
Wayne

November 6
James
Karen
Thomas
Wade
William

November 7
Ada
Dennis
Dorothy
John
John H.

November 8
Christoffer
James
John
Kleber
Margaret
Vincent
Zoe

November 9
Brian
Christopher
Edward
John

Lisa
Patrick

November 10
Alfred
Brian
John
Stephen
Steven
Yang

November 11
Carlos
George
Michael
Myrna
Paul

November 12
Brendan
Clinton
Gerard
Gregory
James
Paul
Richard

November 13
Alfred
Ganesh
José
Joseph
Joseph J.
Laurence
Leo
Lukasz
Samantha

November 14
Clarin
Daniel
Jeffrey
Katherine
Robert

William
Zandra

November 15
Aaron
Barbara
Christina
Gavin
Jaime
Joseph
Joseph F.
Lacey
Lee
Linda
Rochelle
Stephen
Timothy
Thomas J.

November 16
Andrew
Christopher
Dennis
Donald
Faina
Frances
Michael
Robert
Shelley

November 17
Bradley
Charles
Eric
Frank
John
John P.
Luis
Steven
Thomas
Wanda

November 18
Alan

Carlos
James
Julie
Julio
Margaret
Mary
Richard
Robert
Sandra
Theodoros
Timothy
William
Hijacker

November 19
Alexander
Kazushige
Luke
Mary
Michael
Rachel

November 20
Catherine
Hardai
John
Kermit
Kirsten
Michael
Susan
Titus
Vincent

November 21
Catherine
Daniel
Gerald
Jeffrey
Martin
Susan
Hijacker

Sagittarius

November 22
Catherine
Gennady
Jeffrey
Lawrence
Lizette
Michael
Patrick
Robert
Thomas

November 23
Eugene
Paul
Steven
Victor

November 24
Alan
Anthony
Brian
Jason
LaShawana
Lynne
Patrick
Todd

November 25
Andrew
Ann
Bennett
Franklyn
Jeffrey
Juan
Michael
Philip
Vincent

November 26
Alejandro
Anthony
CeeCee
Charles
Christopher
Clara
James
José
Katsuyuki
Manuel
Richard
Toyena

November 27
Christopher
Debra
John
Milagros
Nitin
Peter
Thomas
Vishnoo

November 28
Cortz
Joseph
Lawrence
Melissa
Robert
Walter

November 29
Frank
Giann
Harold
James
John
John J.
Matthew
Scott
Thomas
William

November 30
Derek
Michael
Neilie
Nicholas
Paul
Tara
Thomas
Venesha

December 1
Arkady
Brian
Chet
Liam
Peter
William
William R.

December 2
Charles
Cheryl
Donald
George
Joseph
Nathaniel
Pedro
Peter
Robert
Scott
Stephanie
Thomas

December 3
Jamie
Michael

December 4
Ana
Anil
Emeric
Jennifer
Kathleen
Lawrence
Siucheung
Thomas

December 5
Catherine
Michael

December 6
Arturo
Hyun
Juan
Patrick
Patrick J.
Robert
Thomas
Thomas J.

December 7
Cindy
Dennis
Lars
Michele
Steven

December 8
Cecile
Donna
Ivan
James
John
Laurie
Salvatore
Tyrone

December 9
Kathy
Keith
Kenneth
Mark
Myra
Timothy
Thomas

December 10
John
Joseph
Kenneth
Lawrence
Mary
Matthew
Mirna
Nancy

December 11
Carolyn
Eugueni
Fred
Gary
Harry
Hilda
Lloyd
Michael
Robert
Steven

December 12
Jose
Michael
Patricia

December 13
Aida
Florence
Gerard
Hemanth
Michelle
Nicholas
Richard
Stephen
Thomas
Thomas R.

December 14
Anthony
Cynthia
Eric
James
John
Madeline
Martin
Richard

December 15
Claudia
David
Denise
Emmanuel
Stephen
Taimour
Yvonne

December 16
Dinah
Geoffrey
Gregory
Harshad
Joyce
Lester
Linda
Mukul
Peter
Raymond
William

December 17
Christopher
David
Lorisa
Scott

December 18
George
Jason
Karen
Salvatore
Sean

December 19
Adam
Brenda
Gregory
Joan
Khang
Peter
Robert
Thomas

December 20
Gary
Jason
Jeffrey
Patrick
Rosa
Stephen
Hijacker

December 21
Amy
Daniel
Diane
Eric
Frederick
Jonathan
Joseph
Lisa
Lisa L.
Louis
Ronald

Capricorn

December 22
Amarnauth
Caleb
Daniel
David
Davis
Jeannieann
John
Lisa
Michael
Sharon
Thomas

December 23
Alfred
Barbara
Brian
Carol
Eamon
Eric
Ezra
James
Louis
Manuel
Paul
Pauline
Thomas

December 24
Arnold
Christopher
Donald
Gregorio
John
Joseph
Manuel
Manuel O.
Mark
Michael
Peter
Robin
Roy
See
William

December 25
Albert
Francis
George
Kenneth
Terrance
Thomas

December 26
Craig
David
John
Mary
Maynard
Michael
Monique
Myoung
Paul
W. Ward

December 27
Barbara
Brooke
Lillian
Michael
Michael Joseph
Nasima
Suzanne
Thomas
Timothy

December 28
Andrew
Ann
Brian
Deborah
Francis
Gregory
Joseph
Katie
Margaret
Mohammad
Richard
Robert

December 29
Daniel
Darryl
Helen
John
Michael
Robert
Robert J.

December 30
Abraham
Christopher
David
Howard
Jemal
Karen
Kenneth
Lisa
Lucy
Swarna
William

December 31
Antionette
Bojan
Carlos
John
Lawrence
Louis
Luis
Marisa
Todd

January 1
Adel
Chris
Frank
James
Joon
Mary

January 2
Curtis
Jane
John
Joseph
Joseph J.
Olabisi
Paul
Sharon
Vincent

January 3
Bryan
Gopalakrishnan
Hasmukhrai
Jérôme
Rhondelle
Telmo
Thomas

January 4
Adam
Garry
John
Kevin
Rodney
Scott
Shreyas

January 5
Andrew
Antonio
Christopher
Constantine
Daniel
David
Joseph
Kerene
Kieran
Paul
Richard
Salvatore
Thomas
Wayne

January 6
Angela
Anthony
Brian
Christopher
Don
James
Judy
Kevin
Lukas
Marvin
Siew-Nya
Sushil
Vincent
William
Yuguag

January 7
Albert
Eric
Gerard
Jeffrey
Kevin
Michael
Michael K.
Rena

January 8
Andrew
Azucena
Ian
Kenneth
Kum-Kum
Michael
Robert
Rudy
William

January 9
John
José
Joseph
William

January 10
Gilbert
Henry
James
Michael
Michael L.
Walter

January 11
Boyie
Daniel
Edward
Manuel
Marie
Michael
Michael J.
Thierry
Toshiya

January 12
Alexander
Andrew
Graham
Michael
Moises
Rajesh
Robert

January 13
Asia
Daniel
David
Diane
Francis
Glenn
Richard
Ruben
Sean
Shashi

January 14
Abdoul
Lillian
Timothy
Vicki

January 15
Bonnie
Carmen
Charles
Hector
Mark
Martin
Martin E.
Michael
Paul

January 16
Alexander
Barry
John
Matthew
Michael
Michael W.
Robert
Rocco
Rocco A.
Sandra

January 17
John
Kevin
Maurice
William

January 18
Angela
Debra
Denis
Ehtesham
Israel
Kevin
Michell
Richard
Susan
Timothy
Thomas

January 19
Irina
Jeff
Martha
Michael
Richard
Ronald

Aquarius

January 20
Annette
Benito
Brendan
Mark
Michael
Neil
Thomas

January 21
Alfred
Cesar
Dwight
George
Hugo
Jeffrey
Steven
Yeneneh

January 22
Keithroy
Peter
Susan
William

January 23
Gene
John
Juan
Norman
Rosa
Shuyin

January 24
Allan
Gerard
Howard
John
Peter
Thomas

January 25
Donald
Edward
Edward H.
Edward J.
Francisco
John
John P.
Pablo
Patricia
Robert
Ronald
Vladimir

January 26
Andrew
Antonio
Cesar
Christopher
Doris
Elvin
Federick
George
Nancy
Thomas

January 27
Donald
Mary
Patrick
Phillip
Stephen

January 28
Alejandro
Charles
Jasper
Joseph
Thomas

January 29
Daniel
Frank
Kevin
Patrick
Robert
Salvatore

January 30
David
Dennis
Francis
Jeffrey
Joshua
Michel
Michel P.
Robert
Sareve

January 31
Alberto
Dennis
Gary
Joseph
Kaleen
Laura
Lawrence
Lisa
Patrick
Paul
Randall
Vincent

February 1
Abdoulaye
Abul
Bon
Jayceryll
Jonathan
Kelly
Marc
Michael
Paul
Peter
Thelma

February 2
Andrea

Canfield
Christopher
David
Donald
Ignatius
Pamela
Peter
Steve
Yeshavant
Hijacker

February 3
Balewa
Daniel
Domenick
James
James J.
Joao
John
R. Mark
Todd

February 4
Christopher
Donald
Jonathan
Larry
Mayra
Michael
Ronald
Steven
Thomas

February 5
Betty
Debra
Hebert
James
James J.
Morton
Nauka
Paul
Pedro

February 6
Angelene

Brett
Francois
Gary
George
Hamidou
John
Joseph
Michael
William

February 7
Craig
Dan
Dominick
Gregory
Joseph
Juan
Kimberly
Linda
Peter
Shannon

February 8
Antonio
Carlos
David
Joann
John
Karen
Kenneth
Manuel
Sarah
William

February 9
Clyde
Eliezer
Evelyn
Francis
Joseph
Keith
Leonard
Richard
Robert
Rufino
Sadie

Stephen

February 10
Edward
Edwin
Francis
Frank
James
Karleton
Kevin
Marian
Marina

February 11
David
Dennis
Donald
Edward
Mary
Robert

February 12
Dianne
Gregory
James
Joseph
Joseph M.
Marc
Nancy
Richard
Shannon
Theresa

February 13
Alan
Andrew
John
Leonard
Patricia
Thomas
Walwyn

February 14
Andrew
Carlos
David

Gina
Jeffrey
Larry
Louis
Maile
Michael
Moira
Nicholas
Robert
Rose
Scott
Sita
Timothy
Timothy P.

February 15
John
Kenneth
Sean
Todd

February 16
Debra
John
Mary
Michael
Michael G.
Thomas

February 17
Dennis
Nancy
Simon
William

February 18
Antoinette
Clement
John
Maurita
Michael
Richard
Sophia

Pisces

February 19
Brenda
Charles
Chow
Christopher
Crossley
Eileen
Jim
Manuel
Mark
Michael
Rufino
Thomas

February 20
Andrew
David
Christian
Larry
Marianne
Maudlyn
Michael
Michael B.
Philip
Rodney

February 21
Celeste
Gary
Gerard
James
John

John P.
Matthew
Michael
Michele
Patrick
Robert

February 22
Brenda
Christine
Damion
Karen
Karen Sue
Rahma
Steven

February 23
Donna
Ervin
Guy
John
John D.
Martin
Michael
Ruben
Tatiana
Terence
Thomas

February 24
Brian
Charles

John
John R.
Mark
Whitfield

February 25
Andre
Barbara
David
Joseph
Nigel
Patrick
Richard
Stephen
Timothy
Timothy S.

February 26
DaJuan
Daniel
Douglas
Grace
Hweidar
James
Richard
Syed
Ted
Vincent

February 27
David
Geoffrey

John
Mandy
Michael
Peggie
Timothy

February 28
Alan
Eskedar
Eugen
Ira
John
Kenneth
Neil

February 29
Bradley
Catherine

March 1
Anna
Carlos
Charles
David
Edward
Elvira
Robert
Robert M.
Warren

March 2
Calvin

Herman
Jane
John
Joseph
Mark
Mark J.
Orio
Robert
Sal
Sandra
Sharon
Sheryl
Timothy
Troy

March 3
Fredric
Philip
Suzanne

March 4
Amenia
Claude
Daphne
Frederic
Marianne
Nehamon
Nicole
Sean

March 5
Candace
Dana
Danny
Douglas
Jonathan
Timothy

March 6
Corina
Felix
Jimmy

John
Joseph
Marlyn
Richard
Virgin
William

March 7
Andrew
Andrew C.
W. David
Farrell
John
Kevin
Nobuhiro
Richard

March 8
Anne
Brian
Bruce
Derrick
Isaias
Robert
Sean

March 9
David
Greg
Joshua
Michael
Norberto
Thomas
William

March 10
Jacqueline
Jon
Meta
Terrence
William

March 11
Donna
George
Gerard
James
Joseph
Lee
Mary
Mitchel
Robert

March 12
Dorothy
Gerald
Jennifer
Ronald
Thomas

March 13
Carol
Colleen
Deborah
Klaus
Vincent

March 14
David
Edward
Frank
Kathryn
Michael
Pamela
Rosemarie

March 15
John
Joseph
Mark
Melanie
Robert

March 16
Charles
John
Patrick
Philip
Robert
William

March 17
Gerard
Gregory
John
Mario
Narender
Nicholas
Patricia
Salvatore
Steven
Thomas

March 18
David
Dominique
James
Jose
Joseph

March 19
Alan
Dwayne
Joseph
Renee
Thomas
Hijacker

March 20
Lorenzo
Paula
Peter
Richard
Willie

The Flights and Those Aboard

American Airlines Flight 11

Flight 11 departed Boston Logan International Airport bound for Los Angeles.
It was flown into the North Tower.
Following are the names of those who died aboard American Airlines Flight 11.

CREW

Barbara Arestegui, 38, Marstons Mills, MA
October 21, 1962

Jeffrey Collman, 41, Novato, CA
September 28, 1959

Sara Low, 28, Batesville, AR
October 27, 1972

Karen A. Martin, 40, Danvers, MA
December 18, 1960

Thomas McGuinness, 42, Portsmouth, NH
September 8, 1959

Kathleen Nicosia, 54, Winthrop, MA
June 26, 1947

John Ogonowski, 52, Dracut, MA
February 24, 1951

Betty Ong, 45, Andover, MA
February 5, 1956

Jean Roger, 24, Longmeadow, MA
June 28, 1977

Dianne Snyder, 42, Westport, MA
February 12, 1959

Madeline Sweeney, 35, Acton, MA
December 14, 1965

PASSENGERS

Anna Williams Allison, 48, Stoneham, MA
September 30, 1952

David Angell, 54, Pasadena, CA
April 10, 1947
Mary Lynn Angell, 45, Pasadena, CA
August 11, 1949

Seima Aoyama, 48, Culver City, CA
August 28, 1953

Myra Aronson, 52, Charlestown, MA
December 9, 1950

Christine Barbuto, 32, Brookline, MA
October 28, 1968

Carolyn Beug, 48, Los Angeles, CA
December 11, 1952

Kelly Ann Booms, 24, Brookline, MA
February 1, 1977

Carol Bouchard, 43, Warwick, RI
June 23, 1958

Neilie Anne Heffernan Casey, 32, Wellesley, MA
November 30, 1968

Jeffrey Coombs, 42, Abington, MA
September 18, 1958

Tara Creamer, 30, Worcester, MA
November 30, 1970

Thelma Cuccinello, 71, Wilmot, NH
February 1, 1930

Patrick Currivan, 52, Winchester, MA
September 28, 1948

Brian Dale, 43, Warren, NJ
October 23, 1957

David DiMeglio, 22, Wakefield, MA
August 24, 1979

Donald Americo DiTullio, 49, Peabody, MA
July 3, 1952

Alberto Dominguez, 66, Sydney, Australia
January 31, 1935

Paige Farley-Hackel, 46, Newton, MA
June 7, 1955

Alex Filipov, 70, Concord, MA
April 11, 1931

Carol Flyzik, 40, Plaistow, NH
March 13, 1961

Paul Friedman, 45, New York, NY
August 13, 1956

Karleton D.B. Fyfe, 31, Brookline, MA
February 10, 1970

Peter Gay, 54, Tewksbury, MA
December 16, 1946

Linda George, 27, Westboro, MA
June 11, 1974

Edmund Glazer, 41, Los Angeles, CA
March 21, 1960

Lisa Fenn Gordenstein, 41, Needham, MA
October 1, 1959

Andrew Peter Charles Curry Green, 34, Santa Monica, CA
March 22, 1967

Peter Hashem, 40, Tewksbury, MA
March 20, 1961

Robert Hayes, 37, from Amesbury, MA
October 2, 1963

Edward (Ted) R. Hennessy, 35, Belmont, MA
March 1, 1966

John A. Hofer, 45, Los Angeles, CA
June 15, 1956

Cora Hidalgo Holland, 52, of Sudbury, MA
May 2, 1949

John Nicholas Humber, 60, of Newton, MA,
June 26, 1941

Waleed Iskandar, 34, London, England
August 25, 1967

John Charles Jenkins, 45, Cambridge, MA
January 24, 1956

Charles Edward Jones, 48, Bedford, MA
November 4, 1952

Robin Kaplan, 33, Westboro, MA
May 15, 1968

Barbara Keating, 72, Palm Springs, CA
December 23, 1928

David P. Kovalcin, 42, Hudson, NH
July 25, 1959

Judith Larocque, 50, Framingham, MA
October 27, 1950

Natalie Janis Lasden, 46, Peabody, MA
April 19, 1955

Daniel John Lee, 34, Van Nuys, CA
January 29, 1968

Daniel C. Lewin, 31, Charlestown, MA
May 14, 1970

Susan A. MacKay, 44, Westford, MA
September 4, 1957

Christopher D. Mello, 25, Boston, MA
June 22, 1976

Jeff Mladenik, 43, Hinsdale, IL
June 21, 1958

Antonio Jesús Montoya Valdes, 46, East Boston, MA
January 26, 1954

Carlos Alberto Montoya, 36, Bellmont, MA
March 1, 1965

Laura Lee Morabito, 34, Framingham, MA
October 4, 1966

Mildred Rose Naiman, 81, Andover, MA
March 24, 1920

Laurie Ann Neira, 48, Los Angeles, CA
December 8, 1952

Renee Newell, 37, Cranston, RI
March 19, 1964

Jacqueline J. Norton, 61, Lubec, ME
June 30, 1940

Robert Grant Norton, 85, Lubec, ME
May 11, 1916

Jane M. Orth, 49, Haverhill, MA
March 2, 1952

Thomas Pecorelli, 31, Los Angeles, CA
October 8, 1970

Berinthia Berenson Perkins, 53, Los Angeles, CA
April 14, 1948

Sonia Morales Puopolo, 58, of Dover, MA
August 9, 1939

David E. Retik, 33, Needham, MA
May 23, 1968

Philip M. Rosenzweig, 47, Acton, MA
September 9, 1954

Richard Ross, 58, Newton, MA
April 26, 1943

Jessica Sachs, 22, Billerica, MA
April 22, 1978

Rahma Salie, 28, Boston, MA
February 22, 1973

Heather Lee Smith, 30, Boston, MA
June 12, 1971

Douglas J. Stone, 54, Dover, NH
February 26, 1947

Dino Xavier Suárez, 41, Chino Hills, CA
March 25, 1960

Michael Theodoridis, 32, Boston, MA
September 22, 1968

James Trentini, 65, Everett, MA
May 24, 1936

Mary Trentini, 67, Everett, MA
February 11, 1934

Pendyala Vamsikrishna, 30, Los Angeles, CA
June 15, 1971

Mary Wahlstrom, 78, Kaysville, UT
April 19, 1923

Kenneth Waldie, 46, Methuen, MA
May 13, 1955

John Wenckus, 46, Torrance, CA
September 4, 1955

Candace Lee Williams, 20, Danbury, CT
March 5, 1981

Christopher Zarba, 47, Hopkinton, MA
September 15, 1953

American Airlines Flight 77

Flight 77 departed Washington Dulles International Airport bound for Los Angeles.
It was crashed into the Pentagon.
Following are the names of those who died aboard American Airlines Flight 77.

CREW

Charles Burlingame, 51, Herndon, VA
September 12, 1949

David M. Charlebois, 39, Washington, DC
August 29,962

Michele Heidenberger, 57, Chevy Chase, MD
July 17, 1949

Jennifer Lewis, 38, Culpeper, VA
October 16, 1963

Kenneth Lewis, 49, Culpeper, VA
February 28, 1952

Renee A. May, 39, Baltimore, MD
May 13, 1962

PASSENGERS

Paul Ambrose, 32, Washington, DC
December 26, 1968

Yeneneh Betru, 35, Burbank, CA
January 21, 1966

Mary Jane (MJ) Booth, 64, Falls Church, VA
November 18, 1936

Bernard Curtis Brown, 11, Washington, DC
June 19, 1990

Suzanne Calley, 42, San Martin, CA
September 17, 1957

William Caswell, 54, Silver Spring, MD
June 22, 1947

Sara Clark, 65, Columbia, MD
April 4, 1936

Asia Cottom, 11, Washington, DC
January 13, 1990

James Debeuneure, 58, Upper Marlboro, MD
August 31, 1943

Rodney Dickens, 11, Washington, DC
February 20, 1990

Eddie Dillard, 54, Alexandria, VA
May 18, 1947

Charles Droz, 52, Springfield, VA
February 19, 1949

Barbara G. Edwards, 58, Las Vegas, NV
April 5, 1943

Charles S. Falkenberg, 45, University Park, MD
July 12, 1956

Dana Falkenberg, 3, University Park, MD
July 21, 1998

Zoe Falkenberg, 8, University Park, MD
November 8, 1992

James Joseph Ferguson, 39, Washington, DC
July 23, 1962

Darlene Flagg, 63, Millwood, VA
October 21, 1938

Wilson "Bud" Flagg, 63, Millwood, VA
October 26, 1938

Richard Gabriel, 54, Great Falls, VA
December 13, 1946

Ian J. Gray, 55, Columbia, MD
September 1, 1946

Stanley Hall, 68, Rancho Palos Verdes, CA
April 14, 1933

Bryan Jack, 48, Alexandria, VA
January 3, 1953

Steven D. Jacoby, 43, Alexandria, VA
December 11, 1957

Ann Judge, 49, Great Falls, VA
December 28, 1951

Chandler Keller, 29, El Segundo, CA
October 8, 1971

Yvonne Kennedy, 62, Sydney, New South Wales, Australia
June 29, 1939

Norma Khan, 45, Reston, VA
April 23, 1956

Karen A. Kincaid, 40, Washington, DC
November 3, 1960

Dong Lee, 48, Leesburg, VA
March 30, 1953

Dora Menchaca, 45, of Santa Monica, CA
June 6, 1956

Christopher Newton, 38, Anaheim, CA
September 23, 1962

Barbara Olson, 45, Great Falls, VA
December 27, 1955

Ruben Ornedo, 39, Los Angeles, CA
October 15, 1961

Robert Penniger, 63, of Poway, CA
October 23, 1937

Robert R. Ploger, 59, Annandale, VA
December 19, 1941

Zandra Ploger, 48, Annandale, VA
November 14, 1952

Lisa J. Raines, 42, Great Falls, VA
December 30, 1958

Todd Reuben, 40, Potomac, MD
June 30, 1961

John Sammartino, 37, Annandale, VA
November 8, 1963

Diane Simmons, 52, Great Falls, VA
January 13, 1949

George Simmons, 57, Great Falls, VA
July 16, 1944

Mari-Rae Sopper, 35, Santa Barbara, CA
June 19, 1966

Robert Speisman, 47, Irvington, NY
August 9, 1953

Norma Lang Steuerle, 54, Alexandria, VA
May 1, 1947

Hilda E. Taylor, 62, Forestville, MD
March 31, 1943

Leonard Taylor, 44, Reston, VA
August 20, 1957

Sandra Teague, 31, Fairfax, VA
June 19, 1970

Leslie A. Whittington, 45, University Park, MD
November 3, 1955

John D. Yamnicky, 71, Waldorf, MD
June 8, 1930

Vicki Yancey, 43, Springfield, VA
January 14, 1957

Shuyin Yang, 61, Beijing, China
January 23, 1939

Yuguag Zheng, 65, Beijing, China
January 6, 1936

United Airlines Flight 93

Flight 93 departed Newark International Airport (later renamed Newark Liberty International Airport) bound for San Francisco. It crashed in Shanksville, Pennsylvania.
Following are the names of those who died aboard United Airlines Flight 93.

CREW

Lorraine G. Bay, 58, East Windsor, NJ
July 20, 1943

Sandra W. Bradshaw, 38, Greensboro, NC
June 13, 1963

Jason Dahl, 43, Denver, CO
November 2, 1957

Wanda Anita Green, 49, Linden, NJ
August 22, 1952

Leroy Homer, 36, Marlton, NJ
August 27, 1965

CeeCee Lyles, 33, Fort Myers, FL
November 26, 1967

Deborah Welsh, 49, New York, NY
July 20, 1952

PASSENGERS

Christian Adams, 37, Biebelsheim, Germany
May 27, 1964

Todd Beamer, 32, Cranbury, NJ
November 24, 1968

Alan Beaven, 48, Oakland, CA
October 15, 1952

Mark K. Bingham, 31, San Francisco, CA
May 22, 1970

Deora Frances Bodley, 20, San Diego, CA
April 8, 1981

Marion Britton, 53, New York, NY
April 28, 1948

Thomas E. Burnett, Jr., 38, San Ramon, CA
May 29, 1963

William Cashman, 57, North Bergen, NJ
March 6, 1941

Georgine Rose Corrigan, 56, Honolulu, HI
April 24, 1946

Patricia Cushing, 69, Bayonne, NJ
February 13, 1932

Joseph Deluca, 52, Ledgewood, NJ
April 5, 1949

Patrick Joseph Driscoll, 70, Manalapan, NJ
December 6, 1930

Edward P. Felt, 41, Matawan, NJ
November 9, 1959

Jane C. Folger, 73, Bayonne, NJ
June 12, 1928

Colleen Laura Fraser, 51, Elizabeth, NJ
July 29, 1950

Andrew Garcia, 62, Portola Valley, CA
August 29, 1939

Jeremy Glick, 31, Hewlett, NJ
September 3, 1970

Lauren Grandcolas, 38, San Rafael, CA
August 31, 1963

Donald F. Greene, 52, Greenwich, CT
May 21, 1948

Linda Gronlund, 46, Warwick, NY
September 13, 1954

Richard Guadagno, 38, of Eureka, CA
September 26, 1963

Toshiya Kuge, 20, Nishimidoriguoska, Japan
January 11, 1981

Hilda Marcin, 79, Budd Lake, NJ
December 11, 1921

Nicole Miller, 21, San Jose, CA
March 4, 1980

Louis J. Nacke, 42, New Hope, PA
September 9, 1959

Donald Arthur Peterson, 66, Spring Lake, NJ
April 26, 1935

Jean Hoadley Peterson, 55, Spring Lake, NJ
May 20, 1946

Waleska Martinez, 37, Jersey City, NJ
October 15, 1963

Mark Rothenberg, 52, Scotch Plains, NJ
February 24, 1949

Christine Snyder, 32, Kailua, HI
August 12, 1969

John Talignani, 72, New York, NY
August 31, 1927

Honor Elizabeth Wainio, 27, Watchung, NJ
October 8, 1973

Olga Kristin Gould White, 65, New York, NY
August 29, 1936

United Airlines Flight 175

Flight 175 departed Boston Logan International Airport bound for Los Angeles.
It was flown into the South Tower.
Following are the names of those who died aboard United Airlines Flight 175.

CREW

Robert Fangman, 33, Claymont, DE
March 11, 1968

Michael R. Horrocks, 38, Glen Mills, PA
March 24, 1963

Amy N. Jarret, 28, North Smithfield, RI
October 3, 1972

Amy R. King, 29, Stafford Springs, CT
October 20, 1971

Kathryn L. LaBorie, 44, Providence, RI
March 14, 1957

Alfred Gilles Padre Joseph Marchand, 44, Alamogordo, NM
November 13, 1956

Capt. Victor Saracini, 51, Lower Makefield Township, PA
August 29, 1950

Michael C. Tarrou, 38, Stafford Springs, CT
December 26, 1962

Alicia Nicole Titus, 28, San Francisco, CA
June 11, 1973

PASSENGERS

Alona Abraham, 30, Ashdod, Israel
June 21, 1971

Garnet Edward (Ace) Bailey, 54, Lynnfield, MA
June 13, 1948

Mark Bavis, 31, West Newton, MA
March 31, 1970

Graham Andrew Berkeley, 37, Boston, MA
January 12, 1964

Touri Bolourchi, 69, Beverly Hills, CA
June 10, 1932

Klaus Bothe, 31, Linkenheim, Baden-Wurttemberg, Germany
March 13, 1970

Daniel R. Brandhorst, 41, Los Angeles, CA
June 22, 1960

David Reed Gamboa Brandhorst, 3, Los Angeles, CA
June 23, 1998

John Brett Cahill, 56, Wellesley, MA
April 20, 1945

Christoffer Carstanjen, 33, Turner Falls, MA
November 8, 1967

John (Jay) J. Corcoran, 43, Norwell, MA
October 2, 1957

Dorothy Alma De Araujo, 80, Long Beach, CA
November 7, 1920

Ana Gloria Pocasangre de Barrera, 49, San Salvador, El Salvador
July 13, 1952

Lisa Frost, 22, Rancho Santa Margarita, CA
December 21, 1978

Ronald Gamboa, 33, Los Angeles, CA
April 30, 1968

Lynn Catherine Goodchild, 25, Attleboro, MA
May 27, 1976

Peter Morgan Goodrich, 33, Sudbury, MA
October 1, 1967

Douglas A. Gowell, 52, Methuen, MA
September 30, 1948

The Reverend Francis E. Grogan, 76, of Easton, MA
January 13, 1925

Carl Max Hammond, 37, Derry, NH
October 4, 1963

Christine Lee Hanson, 2, Groton, MA
February 22, 1999

Peter Hanson, 32, Groton, MA
January 24, 1969

Sue Kim Hanson, 35, Groton, MA
July 28, 1966

Gerald F. Hardacre, 61, Carlsbad, CA
November 21, 1939

Eric Samadikan Hartono, 20, Boston, MA
December 23, 1981

James E. Hayden, 47, Westford, MA
March 29, 1954

Herbert W. Homer, 48, Milford, MA
February 5, 1953

Robert Adrien Jalbert, 61, Swampscott, MA
September 9, 1940

Ralph Francis Kershaw, 52, Manchester-by-the-Sea, MA
April 8, 1949

Heinrich Kimmig, 43, Willstaett, Germany
July 26, 1958

Brian Kinney, 29, Lowell, MA
June 7, 1973

Robert George LeBlanc, 70, Lee, NH
October 28, 1930

Maclovio Lopez, Jr., 41, Norwalk, CA
April 29, 1960

Marianne MacFarlane, 34, Revere, MA
February 20, 1967

Louis Neil Mariani, 59, Derry, NH
December 23, 1942

Juliana Valentine McCourt, 4, New London, CT
May 4, 1997

Ruth Magdaline McCourt, 45, New London, CT
June 4, 1956

Wolfgang Peter Menzel, 59, Wilhelmshaven, Germany
November 1, 1941

Shawn M. Nassaney, 25, Pawtucket, RI
July 7, 1976

Marie Pappalardo, 53, Paramount, CA
October 12, 1947

Patrick Quigley, 40, of Wellesley, MA
February 25, 1961

Frederick Charles Rimmele, 32, Marblehead, MA
October 3, 1968

James M. Roux, 43, Portland, ME
July 29, 1958

Jesús Sanchez, 45, Hudson, MA
March 21, 1956

Mary Kathleen Shearer, 61, Dover, NH
March 11, 1940

Robert Michael Shearer, 63, Dover, NH
March 1, 1938

Jane Louise Simpkin, 36, Wayland, MA
March 28, 1965

Brian D. Sweeney, 38, Barnstable, MA
August 10, 1963

Deborah Tavolarella, 36, Dedham, MA
March 21, 1955

Timothy Ward, 38, San Diego, CA
February 14, 1963

William M. Weems, 46, Marblehead, MA
August 2, 1955

The Buildings

The Pentagon

Following are the names of those who died at the Pentagon, listed alphabetically by last name.

Spc. Craig Amundson, 28, Fort Belvoir, VA
August 21, 1973

Melissa Rose Barnes, 27, Redlands, CA
November 28, 1973

(Retired) Master Sgt. Max Beilke, 69, Laurel, MD
July 24, 1932

Kris Romeo Bishundat, 23, Waldorf, MD
September 14, 1977

Carrie Blagburn, 48, Temple Hills, MD
July 1, 1953

Lt. Col. Canfield D. Boone, 54, Clifton, VA
February 2, 1948

Donna Bowen, 42, Waldorf, MD
December 8, 1958

Allen Boyle, 30, Fredericksburg, VA
October 3, 1970

Christopher Lee Burford, 23, Hubert, NC
October 4, 1977

Daniel Martin Caballero, 21, Houston, TX
November 21, 1979

Sgt. 1st Class José Orlando Calderon-Olmedo, 44, Annandale, VA
August 27, 1957

Angelene C. Carter, 51, Forrestville, MD
February 6, 1950

Sharon Carver, 38, Waldorf, MD
March 2, 1963

John J. Chada, 55, Manassas, VA
September 13, 1945

Rosa Maria (Rosemary) Chapa, 64, Springfield, VA
April 6, 1938

Julian Cooper, 39, Springdale, MD
April 20, 1962

Lt. Cmdr. Eric Allen Cranford, 32, Drexel, NC
December 21, 1968

Ada M. Davis, 57, Camp Springs, MD
November 7, 1943

Capt. Gerald Francis Deconto, 44, Sandwich, MA
August 17, 1957

Lt. Col. Jerry Don Dickerson, 41, Durant, MS
July 29, 1960

Johnnie Doctor, 32, Jacksonville, FL
October 21, 1968

Capt. Robert Edward Dolan, 43, Alexandria, VA
March 1, 1958

Cmdr. William Howard Donovan, 37, Nunda, NY
May 15, 1964

Cmdr. Patrick S. Dunn, 39, Springfield, VA
January 31, 1962

Edward Thomas Earhart, 26, Salt Lick, KY
May 14, 1975

Lt. Cmdr. Robert Randolph Elseth, 37, Vestal, NY
December 2, 1964

Jamie Lynn Fallon, 23, Woodbridge, VA
December 3, 1977

Amelia V. Fields, 36, Dumfries, VA
September 11, 1955

Gerald P. Fisher, 57, Potomac, MD
March 28, 1944

Matthew Michael Flocco, 21, Newark, DE
November 29, 1979

Sandra N. Foster, 41, Clinton, MD
June 10, 1960

Capt. Lawrence Daniel Getzfred, 57, Elgin, NE
May 29, 1944

Cortz Ghee, 54, Reisterstown, MD
November 28, 1947

Brenda C. Gibson, 59, Falls Church, VA
February 22, 1942

Ron Golinski, 60, Columbia, MD
June 30, 1941

Diane M. Hale-McKinzy, 38, Alexandria, VA
December 21, 1962

Carolyn B. Halmon, 49, Washington, DC
March 27, 1952

Sheila Hein, 51, University Park, MD
May 2, 1950

Ronald John Hemenway, 37, Shawnee, KS.
July 25, 1964

Maj. Wallace Cole Hogan, 40, FL
October 9, 1960

Jimmie Ira Holley, 54, Lanham, MD
August 1, 1947

Angela Houtz, 27, La Plata, MD
September 6, 1974

Brady K. Howell, 26, Arlington, VA
April 4, 1975

Peggie Hurt, 36, Crewe, VA
February 27, 1965

Lt. Col. Stephen Neil Hyland, 45, Burke, VA
November 10, 1954

Robert J. Hymel, 55, Woodbridge, VA
August 13, 1946

Sgt. Maj. Lacey B. Ivory, 43, Woodbridge, VA
November 15, 1958

Lt. Col. Dennis M. Johnson, 48, Port Edwards, WI
April 1, 1953

Judith Jones, 53, Woodbridge, VA
July 24, 1948

Brenda Kegler, 49, Washington, DC
December 19, 1951

Lt. Michael Scott Lamana, 31, Baton Rouge, LA
July 6, 1970

David W. Laychak, 40, Manassas, VA
January 13, 1961

Samantha Lightbourn-Allen, 36, Hillside, MD
November 13, 1964

Maj. Steve Long, 39, GA
March 29, 1962

James T. Lynch, 55, Manassas, VA
July 4, 1946

Terence M. Lynch, 49, Alexandria, VA
September 5, 1952

Nehamon Lyons, 30, Mobile, AL
March 4, 1971

Shelley A. Marshall, 37, Marbury, MD
November 16, 1963

Teresa Martin, 45, Stafford, VA
August 21, 1956

Ada L. Mason-Acker, 50, Springfield, VA
June 20, 1951

Lt. Col. Dean E. Mattson, 57, CA
March 30, 1944

Lt. Gen. Timothy J. Maude, 53, Fort Myer, VA
November 18, 1947

Robert J. Maxwell, 53, Manassas, VA
June 14, 1948

Molly McKenzie, 38, Dale City, VA
April 8, 1963

Patricia E. (Patti) Mickley, 41, Springfield, VA
October 15, 1959

Maj. Ronald D. Milam, 33, Washington, DC
August 11, 1968

Gerard (Jerry) P. Moran, 39, Upper Marlboro, MD
December 13, 1961

Odessa V. Morris, 54, Upper Marlboro, MD
July 11, 1947

Brian Anthony Moss, 34, Sperry, OK
October 28, 1966

Ted Moy, 48, Silver Spring, MD
February 26, 1953

Lt. Cmdr. Patrick Jude Murphy, 38, Flossmoor, IL
June 25, 1963

Khang Nguyen, 41, Fairfax, VA
December 19, 1959

Michael Allen Noeth, 30, New York, NY
July 7, 1971

Diana Borrero de Padro, 55, Woodbridge, VA
August 11, 1946

Spc. Chin Sun Pak, 25, Woodbridge, VA
September 13, 1976

Lt. Jonas Martin Panik, 26, Mingoville, PA
November 1, 1974

Maj. Clifford L. Patterson, 33, Alexandria, VA
July 2, 1968

Lt. J.G. Darin Howard Pontell, 26, Columbia, MD
August 24, 1975

Scott Powell, 35, Silver Spring, MD
June 20, 1966

(Retired) Capt. Jack Punches, 51, Clifton, VA
April 16, 1951

Joseph John Pycior, 39, Carlstadt, NJ
October 14, 1961

Deborah Ramsaur, 45, Annandale, VA
July 2, 1956

Rhonda Sue Rasmussen, 44, Woodbridge, VA
October 18, 1956

Marsha Dianah Ratchford, 34, Prichard, AL
May 26, 1967

Martha Reszke, 36, Stafford, VA
January 19, 1945

CeCelia E. Richard, 41, Fort Washington, MD
June 2, 1960

Edward V. Rowenhorst, 32, Lake Ridge, VA
April 19, 1969

Judy Rowlett, 44, Woodbridge, VA
May 8, 1957

Robert E. Russell, 52, Oxon Hill, MD
April 29, 1949

William R. Ruth, 57, Mount Airy, MD
November 29, 1943

Charles E. Sabin, 54, Burke, VA
July 31, 1947

Marjorie C. Salamone, 53, Springfield, VA
October 7, 1947

Lt. Col. David M. Scales, 44, Cleveland, OH
September 27, 1956

Cmdr. Robert Allan Schlegel, 38, Alexandria, VA
June 6, 1963

Janice Scott, 46, Springfield, VA
October 12, 1954

Michael L. Selves, 53, Fairfax, VA
September 16, 1947

Marian Serva, 47, Stafford, VA
April 30, 1954

Cmdr. Dan Frederic Shanower, 40, Naperville, IL
February 7, 1961

Antionette Sherman, 35, Forest Heights, MD
December 31, 1965

Don Simmons, 58, Dumfries, VA
January 6, 1943

Cheryle D. Sincock, 53, Dale City, VA
April 22, 1948

Gregg Harold Smallwood, 44, Overland Park, KS
July 30, 1957

(Retired) Lt. Col. Gary F. Smith, 55, Alexandria, VA
October 9, 1945

Patricia J. Statz, 41, Takoma Park, MD
January 25, 1960

Edna L. Stephens, 53, Washington, DC
April 19, 1948

Sgt. Maj. Larry Strickland, 52, Woodbridge, VA
February 14, 1949

Maj. Kip P. Taylor, 38, McLean, VA
September 5, 1963

Sandra C. Taylor, 50, Alexandria, VA
October 8, 1950

Karl W. Teepe, 57, Centreville, VA
September 24, 1943

Sgt. Tamara Thurman, 25, Brewton, AL
April 15, 1976

Lt. Cmdr. Otis Vincent Tolbert, 38, Lemoore, CA
September 29, 1962

Willie Q. Troy, 51, Aberdeen, MD
March 20, 1950

Lt. Cmdr. Ronald James Vauk, 37, Nampa, ID
January 25, 1964

Lt. Col. Karen Wagner, 40, Houston, TX
February 22, 1961

Meta L. Waller, 60, Alexandria, VA
March 10, 1941

Staff Sgt. Maudlyn A. White, 38, St. Croix, Virgin Islands
February 20, 1963

Sandra L. White, 44, Dumfries, VA
September 18, 1956

Ernest M. Willcher, 62, North Potomac, MD
October 23, 1938

Lt. Cmdr. David Lucian Williams, 32, Newport, OR
February 2, 1969

Maj. Dwayne Williams, 40, Jacksonville, AL
March 19, 1961

Marvin R. Woods, 57, Great Mills, MD
January 6, 1944

Kevin Wayne Yokum, 27, Lake Charles, LA
October 7, 1973

Donald McArthur Young, 41, Roanoke, VA
September 21, 1959

Edmond Young, 22, Owings, MD
May 22, 1979

Lisa L. Young, 36, Germantown, MD
December 21, 1963

The World Trade Center

Following are the names of those who died at the World Trade Center, New York, on September 11, 2001, listed alphabetically by last name.

A

Gordon McCannel Aamoth, 32, New York, NY
August 8, 1969

Maria Rose Abad, 49, Syosset, NY
June 10, 1952

Edelmiro (Ed) Abad, 54, New York, NY
September 13, 1946

Andrew Anthony Abate, 37, Melville, NY
September 6, 1964

Vincent Abate, 40, New York, NY
May 23, 1961

Laurence Christopher Abel, 37, New York, NY
October 28, 1963

William F. Abrahamson, 58, Cortland Manor, NY
March 16, 1943

Richard Anthony Aceto, 42, Wantagh, NY
March 24, 1959

Erica Van Acker, 62, New York, NY
April 9, 1939

Heinrich B. Ackermann, 38, New York, NY
November 4, 1962

Paul Andrew Acquaviva, 29, Glen Rock, NJ
October 24, 1971

Donald L. Adams, 28, Chatham, NJ
January 27, 1973

Shannon Lewis Adams, 25, New York, NY
February 7, 1976

Stephen Adams, 51, New York, NY
March 23, 1950

Patrick Adams, 60, New York, NY
December 20, 1939

Ignatius Adanga, 62, New York, NY
February 2, 1939

Christy A. Addamo, 28, New Hyde Park, NY
September 24, 1972

Terence E. Adderley, 22, Bloomfield Hills, MI
May 12, 1979

Sophia B. Addo, 36, New York, NY
February 18, 1965

Lee Adler, 48, Springfield, NJ
March 11, 1953

Daniel Thomas Afflitto, 32, Manalapan, NJ
May 4, 1969

Emmanuel Afuakwah, 37, New York, NY
December 15, 1963

Alok Agarwal, 36, Jersey City, NJ
May 3, 1965

Mukul Agarwala, 37, New York, NY
December 16, 1963

Joseph Agnello, 35, New York, NY
October 10, 1965

David Scott Agnes, 46, New York, NY
September 10, 1955

Joao A. Aguiar, Jr., 30, Red Bank, NJ
February 3, 1971

Lt. Brian G. Ahearn, 43, Huntington, NY
March 8, 1958

Jeremiah J. Ahern, 74, Cliffside Park, NJ
September 8, 1927

Joanne Ahladiotis, 27, New York, NY
June 10, 1974

Shabbir Ahmed, 47, New York, NY
August 13, 1954

Terrance Andre Aiken, 30, New York, NY
December 25, 1970

Godwin Ajala, 33, New York, NY
June 9, 1968

Gertrude M. Alagero, 37, New York, NY
September 7, 1964

Andrew Alameno, 37, Westfield, NJ
January 12, 1964

Margaret Ann (Peggy) Alario, 41, New York, NY
September 18, 1959

Gary Albero, 39, Emerson, NJ
June 7, 1962

Jon L. Albert, 46, Upper Nyack, NY
April, 24, 1955

Peter Craig Alderman, 25, New York, NY
August 19, 1976

Jacquelyn Delaine Aldridge-Frederick, 46, New York, NY
October 18, 1954

Grace Alegre Cua, 40, Glen Rock, NJ
February 26, 1961

David D. Alger, 57, New York, NY
December 15, 1943

Ernest Alikakos, 43, New York, NY
June 27, 1958

Edward L. Allegretto, 51, Colonia, NJ
March 14, 1950

Eric Allen, 44, New York, NY
January 7, 1957

Joseph Ryan Allen, 39, New York, NY
February 6, 1962

Richard Lanard Allen, 30, New York, NY
July 10, 1971

Richard Dennis Allen, 31, New York, NY
February 26, 1970

Christopher Edward Allingham, 36, River Edge, NJ
October 6, 1964

Janet M. Alonso, 41, Stony Point, NY
August 14, 1960

Anthony Alvarado, 31, New York, NY
October 23, 1969

Antonio Javier Alvarez, 23, New York, NY
May 12, 1978

Telmo Alvear, 25, New York, NY
January 3, 1976

Cesar A. Alviar, 60, Bloomfield, NJ
January 26, 1941

Tariq Amanullah, 40, Metuchen, NJ
May 1, 1961

Angelo Amaranto, 60, New York, NY
August 1, 1941

James Amato, 43, Ronkonkoma, NY
May 10, 1958

Joseph Amatuccio, 41, New York, NY
March 15, 1960

Christopher Charles Amoroso, 29, New York, NY
June 1, 1972

Kazuhiro Anai, 42, Scarsdale, NY
May 26, 1959

Calixto Anaya, 35, Suffern, NY
June 19, 1966

Joseph Peter Anchundia, 26, New York, NY
May 6, 1975

Kermit Charles Anderson, 57, Green Brook, NJ
November 20, 1943

Yvette Anderson, 53, New York, NY
July 29, 1948

John Andreacchio, 52, New York, NY
March 27, 1949

Michael Rourke Andrews, 34, Belle Harbor, NY
January 10, 1967

Jean A. Andrucki, 42, Hoboken, NJ
October 1, 1957

Siew-Nya Ang, 37, East Brunswick, NJ
January 6, 1964

Joseph Angelini, 63, Lindenhurst, NY
April 11, 1938

Joseph John Angelini, 38, Lindenhurst, NY
August 3, 1963

Laura Angilletta, 23, New York, NY
August 11, 1978

Doreen J. Angrisani, 44, New York, NY
October 29, 1956

Lorraine D. Antigua, 32, Middletown, NJ
September 27, 1968

Peter Paul Apollo, 26, Hoboken, NJ
September 23, 1974

Faustino Apostol, 55, New York, NY
April 15, 1946

Frank Thomas Aquilino, 26, New York, NY
October 16, 1974

Patrick Michael Aranyos, 26, New York, NY
June 25, 1975

David Gregory Arce, 36, New York, NY
July 2, 1965

Michael G. Arczynski, 45, Little Silver, NJ
February 16, 1956

Louis Arena, 32, New York, NY
July 18, 1969

Adam Arias, 37, Staten Island, NY
January 4, 1964

Michael J. Armstrong, 34, New York, NY
August 31, 1967

Jack Charles Aron, 52, Bergenfield, NJ
April 22, 1949

Joshua Aron, 29, New York, NY
June 29, 1972

Richard Avery Aronow, 48, Mahwah, NJ
March 20, 1953

Japhet J. Aryee, 49, Spring Valley, NY
May 1, 1962

Carl Asaro, 39, Middletown, NY
October 10, 1963

Michael A. Asciak, 47, Ridgefield, NJ
May 18, 1954

Michael Edward Asher, 53, Monroe, NY
June 7, 1948

Janice Ashley, 25, Rockville Centre, NY
March 27, 1976

Thomas J. Ashton, 21, New York, NY
December 6, 1979

Manuel O. Asitimbay, 36, New York, NY
December 24, 1965

Lt. Gregg Arthur Atlas, 45, Howells, NY
September 25, 1956

Gerald Atwood, 38, New York, NY
May 28, 1963

James Audiffred, 38, New York, NY
November 29, 1962

Kenneth W. Van Auken, 47, East Brunswick, NJ
August 30, 1954

Louis F. Aversano, Jr., 58, Manalapan, NJ
February 14, 1943

Ezra Aviles, 41, Commack, NY
December 23, 1959

Samuel (Sandy) Ayala, 36, New York, NY
August 5, 1965

B

Arlene T. Babakitis, 47, Secaucus, NJ
October 28, 1953

Eustace (Rudy) Bacchus, 48, Metuchen, NJ
May 20, 1953

John James Badagliacca, 35, New York, NY
July 15, 1966

Jane Ellen Baeszler, 43, New York, NY
January 2, 1958

Robert J. Baierwalter, 44, Albertson, NY
May 7, 1957

Andrew J. Bailey, 29, New York, NY
April 20, 1972

Brett T. Bailey, 28, Bricktown, NJ
February 6, 1973

Tatyana Bakalinskaya, 43, New York, NY
May 21, 1958

Michael S. Baksh, 36, Englewood, NJ
May 18, 1965

Sharon Balkcom, 43, White Plains, NY
January 2, 1958

Michael Andrew Bane, 33, Yardley, PA
April 14, 1968

Kathy Bantis, 44, Chicago, IL
December 9, 1956

Gerard Jean Baptiste, 35, New York, NY
March 11, 1966

Walter Baran, 42, New York, NY
November 28, 1958

Gerard A. Barbara, 53, New York, NY
March 17, 1948

Paul V. Barbaro, 35, Holmdel, NJ
May 27, 1966

James W. Barbella, 53, Oceanside, NY
May 23, 1948

Ivan Kyrillos Fairbanks Barbosa, 30, Jersey City, NJ
May 22, 1971

Victor Daniel Barbosa, 23, New York, NY
July 12, 1978

Colleen Ann Barkow, 26, East Windsor, NJ
March 13, 1975

David Michael Barkway, 34, Toronto, Ontario, Canada
September 8, 1967

Matthew Barnes, 37, Monroe, NY
December 10, 1963

Sheila Patricia Barnes, 55, Bay Shore, NY
March 30, 1946

Evan J. Baron, 38, Bridgewater, NJ
September 25, 1962

Renee Barrett-Arjune, 41, Irvington, NJ
April 24, 1960

Arthur T. Barry, 35, New York, NY
October 22, 1965

Diane G. Barry, 60, New York, NY
July 23, 1941

Maurice Vincent Barry, 49, Rutherford, NJ
September 27, 1962

Scott D. Bart, 28, Malverne, NY
June 7, 1973

Carlton W. Bartels, 44, New York, NY
September 9, 1957

Guy Barzvi, 29, New York, NY
February 23, 1972

Inna Basina, 43, New York, NY
June 26, 1958

Alysia Basmajian, 23, Bayonne, NJ
July 1, 1978

Kenneth William Basnicki, 48, Etobicoke, Ontario, Canada
December 10, 1952

Lt. Steven J. Bates, 42, New York, NY
November 23, 1958

Paul James Battaglia, 22, New York, NY
January 2, 1979

W. David Bauer, 45, Rumson, NJ
March 7, 1956

Ivhan Luis Carpio Bautista, 24, New York, NY
September 11, 1977

Marlyn C. Bautista, 46, Iselin, NJ
May 6, 1955

Jasper Baxter, 45, Philadelphia, PA
January 28, 1956

Michele (Du Berry) Beale, 37, Essex, Britain
June 27, 1964

Paul F. Beatini, 40, Park Ridge, NJ
June 26, 1961

Jane S. Beatty, 53, Belford, NJ
June 2, 1948

Larry I. Beck, 38, Baldwin, NY
February 4, 1963

Manette Marie Beckles, 43, Rahway, NJ
May 19, 1958

Carl John Bedigian, 35, New York, NY
August 31, 1966

Michael Beekman, 39, New York, NY
September 22, 1961

Maria Behr, 41, Milford, NJ
August 15, 1960

Yelena Belilovsky, 38, Mamaroneck, NY
June 28, 1963

Nina Patrice Bell, 39, New York, NY
June 10, 1962

Debbie S. Bellows, 30, East Windsor, NJ
March 25, 1971

Stephen Elliot Belson, 51, New York, NY
May 9, 1950

Paul Michael Benedetti, 32, New York, NY
May 21, 1969

Denise Lenore Benedetto, 40, New York, NY
October 19, 1960

Bryan Craig Bennett, 25, New York, NY
July 29, 1976

Eric L. Bennett, 29, New York, NY
October 17, 1971

Oliver Duncan Bennett, 29, London, England
April 8, 1972

Margaret L. Benson, 52, Rockaway, NJ
August 16, 1949

Dominick J. Berardi, 25, New York, NY
February 7, 1976

James Patrick Berger, 44, Lower Makefield, PA
December 14, 1956

Steven Howard Berger, 45, Manalapan, NJ
February 4, 1956

John P. Bergin, 39, New York, NY
November 10, 1961

Alvin Bergsohn, 48, Baldwin Harbor, NY
June 13, 1953

Daniel D. Bergstein, 38, Teaneck, NJ
October 19, 1962

Michael J. Berkeley, 38, New York, NY
September 11, 1963

Donna M. Bernaerts, 44, Hoboken, NJ
March 11, 1957

David W. Bernard, 57, Chelmsford, MA
October 19, 1944

William Bernstein, 44, New York, NY
January 8, 1957

David M. Berray, 39, New York, NY
October 19, 1961

David S. Berry, 43, New York, NY
May 31, 1958

Joseph J. Berry, 55, Saddle River, NJ
January 28, 1946

William Reed Bethke, 36, Hamilton, NJ
October 7, 1964

Timothy D. Betterly, 42, Little Silver, NJ
December 27, 1958

Edward F. Beyea, 42, New York, NY
July 3, 1959

Paul Michael Beyer, 37, New York, NY
November 12, 1963

Anil T. Bharvaney, 41, East Windsor, NJ
December 4, 1959

Bella Bhukhan, 24, Union, NJ
March 26, 1977

Shimmy D. Biegeleisen, 42, New York, NY
July 21, 1959

Peter Alexander Bielfeld, 44, New York, NY
April 21, 1957

William Biggart, 54, New York, NY
July 20, 1947

Brian Bilcher, 36, New York, NY
December 23, 1963

Carl Vincent Bini, 44, New York, NY
June 28, 1957

Gary Bird, 51, Tempe, AZ
June 23, 1950

Joshua David Birnbaum, 24, New York, NY
June 17, 1977

George Bishop, 52, Granite Springs, NY
April 10, 1949

Jeffrey D. Bittner, 27, New York, NY
January 7, 1974

Balewa Albert Blackman, 26, New York, NY
February 3, 1975

Christopher Joseph Blackwell, 42, Patterson, NY
January 26, 1959

Susan L. Blair, 35, East Brunswick, NJ
May 24, 1966

Harry Blanding, 38, Blakeslee, PA
July 29, 1963

Janice L. Blaney, 55, Williston Park, NY
June 1, 1946

Craig Michael Blass, 27, Greenlawn, NY
February 7, 1974

Rita Blau, 52, New York, NY
June 15, 1949

Richard M. Blood, 38, Ridgewood, NJ
July 25, 1963

Michael A. Boccardi, 30, Bronxville, NY
February 6, 1971

John Paul Bocchi, 38, New Vernon, NJ
March 2, 1963

Michael L. Bocchino, 45, New York, NY
November 25, 1955

Susan Mary Bochino, 36, New York, NY
April 15, 1965

Bruce Douglas (Chappy) Boehm, 49, West
   Hempstead, NY
March 8, 1952

Nicholas A. Bogdan, 34, Browns Mills, NJ
December 13, 1966

Darren C. Bohan, 34, New York, NY
September 29, 1966

Lawrence Francis Boisseau, 36, Freehold, NJ
November 28, 1964

Vincent M. Boland, 25, Ringwood, NJ
August 4, 1976

Alan Bondarenko, 53, Flemington, NJ
November 18, 1947

Andre Bonheur, 40, New York, NY
April 5, 1961

Colin Arthur Bonnett, 39, New York, NY
July 11, 1962

Frank Bonomo, 42, Port Jefferson, NY
August 12, 1959

Yvonne L. Bonomo, 30, New York, NY
December 15, 1970

Sean Booker, 35, Irvington, NJ
January 13, 1966

Sherry Ann Bordeaux, 38, Jersey City, NJ
August 26, 1963

Krystine C. Bordenabe, 33, Old Bridge, NJ
July 28, 1968

Martin Boryczewski, 29, Parsippany, NJ
August 17, 1972

Richard E. Bosco, 34, Suffern, NY
January 19, 1967

John Howard Boulton, 29, New York, NY
November 7, 1971

Francisco Bourdier, 41, New York, NY
September 18, 1960

Thomas H. Bowden, 36, Wyckoff, NJ
September 2, 1965

Kimberly S. Bowers, 31, Islip, NY
February 7, 1970

Veronique (Bonnie) Nicole Bowers, 28, New York, NY
May 23, 1973

Larry Bowman, 46, New York, NY
September 2, 1955

Shawn Edward Bowman, 28, New York, NY
September 16, 1972

Kevin L. Bowser, 45, Philadelphia, PA
March 7, 1956

Gary R. Box, 37, North Bellmore, NY
May 12, 1964

Gennady Boyarsky, 34, New York, NY
November 22, 1966

Pamela Boyce, 43, New York, NY
March 14, 1968

Michael Boyle, 37, Westbury, NY
August 8, 1964

Alfred Braca, 54, Leonardo, NJ
November 10, 1946

Sandra Conaty Brace, 60, New York, NY
November 18, 1940

Kevin H. Bracken, 37, New York, NY
April 25, 1964

David Brian Brady, 41, Summit, NJ
June 10, 1960

Alexander Braginsky, 38, Stamford, CT
May 10, 1963

Nicholas W. Brandemarti, 21, Mantua, NJ
September 26, 1979

Michelle Renee Bratton, 23, Yonkers, NY
April 26, 1978

Patrice Braut, 31, New York, NY
August 8, 1970

Lydia Estelle Bravo, 50, Dunellen, NJ
July 20, 1951

Ronald Michael Breitweiser, 39, Middletown
   Township, NJ
August 4, 1962

Edward A. Brennan, 37, New York, NY
April 28, 1964

Frank H. Brennan, 50, New York, NY
September 25, 1950

Michael Emmett Brennan, 27, New York, NY
November 20, 1973

Peter Brennan, 30, Ronkonkoma, NY
December 24, 1970

Thomas M. Brennan, 32, Scarsdale, NY
December 4, 1968

Capt. Daniel Brethel, 43, Farmingdale, NY
June 11, 1958

Gary L. Bright, 36, Union City, NJ
January 31, 1965

Jonathan Eric Briley, 43, Mount Vernon, NY
March 5, 1958

Mark A. Brisman, 34, Armonk, NY
May 9, 1967

Paul Gary Bristow, 27, New York, NY
January 15, 1974

Victoria Alvarez Brito, 38, New York, NY
March 23, 1963

Mark Francis Broderick, 42, Old Bridge, NJ
September 2, 1961

Herman C. Broghammer, 58, North Merrick, NY
July 7, 1943

Keith Broomfield, 49, New York, NY
August 25, 1952

Janice J. Brown, 35, New York, NY
October 18, 1965

Lloyd Brown, 28, Bronxville, NY
October 23, 1972

Capt. Patrick J. Brown, 48, New York, NY
November 9, 1952

Bettina Browne-Radburn, 49, Atlantic Beach, NY
August 23, 1954

Mark Bruce, 40, Summit, NJ
January 20, 1961

Richard Bruehert, 38, Westbury, NY
February 25, 1963

Andrew Brunn, 28, New York, NY
April 27, 1973

Capt. Vincent Brunton, 43, New York, NY
January 2, 1958

Ronald Paul Bucca, 47, Tuckahoe, NY
May 6, 1954

Brandon J. Buchanan, 24, New York, NY
April 9, 1977

Greg Joseph Buck, 37, New York, NY
March 9, 1964

Dennis Buckley, 38, Chatham, NJ
January 31, 1963

Nancy Bueche, 43, Hicksville, NY
August 10, 1958

Patrick Joseph Buhse, 36, Lincroft, NJ
March 16, 1965

John E. Bulaga, 35, Paterson, NJ
November 7, 1965

Stephen Bunin, 45, New York, NY
August 15, 1957

Matthew J. Burke, 28, New York, NY
March 24, 1973

Thomas Daniel Burke, 38, Bedford Hills, NY
December 13, 1962

Capt. William F. Burke, 46, New York, NY
March 9, 1956

Donald James Burns, 61, Nissequogue, NY
May 3, 1940

Kathleen A. Burns, 49, New York, NY
October 3, 1952

Keith James Burns, 39, East Rutherford, NJ
February 9, 1962

John Patrick Burnside, 36, New York, NY
December 10, 1964

Irina Buslo, 32, New York, NY
October 28, 1968

Milton Bustillo, 37, New York, NY
October 6, 1963

Thomas M. Butler, 37, Kings Park, NY
May 15, 1964

Patrick Byrne, 39, New York, NY
July 22, 1962

Timothy G. Byrne, 36, Manhattan, NY
January 14, 1965

C

Jesús Cabezas, 66, New York, NY
August 30, 1935

Lillian Caceres, 48, New York, NY
January 14, 1953

Brian Joseph Cachia, 26, New York, NY
July 20, 1975

Steven Dennis Cafiero, 31, New York, NY
June 12, 1970

Richard Michael Caggiano, 25, New York, NY
April 27, 1976

Cecile M. Caguicla, 55, Boonton, NJ
December 8, 1945

Michael John Cahill, 37, East Williston, NY
February 18, 1964

Scott Walter Cahill, 30, West Caldwell, NJ
May 27, 1971

Thomas Joseph Cahill, 36, Franklin Lakes, NJ
September 14, 1964

George C. Cain, 35, Massapequa, NY
May 13, 1966

Salvatore B. Calabro, 38, New York, NY
December 8, 1962

Joseph M. Calandrillo, 49, Hawley, PA
February 9, 1952

Philip V. Calcagno, 57, New York, NY
February 20, 1944

Edward Calderon, 44, Jersey City, NJ
July 21, 1957

Kenneth Marcus Caldwell, 30, New York, NY
February 8, 1971

Dominick E. Calia, 40, Manalapan, NJ
June 18, 1961

Felix Bobby Calixte, 38, New York, NY
March 6, 1963

Capt. Francis Joseph Callahan, 51, New York, NY
February 9, 1950

Liam Callahan, 44, Rockaway, NJ
April 18, 1957

Gino Luigi Calvi, 34, East Rutherford, NJ
July 27, 1967

Roko Camaj, 60, Manhasset, NY
August 17, 1941

Michael F. Cammarata, 22, Huguenot, NY
October 5, 1978

David Otey Campbell, 51, Basking Ridge, NJ
June 6, 1950

Geoffrey Thomas Campbell, 31, New York, NY
December 16, 1969

Jill Mauer-Campbell, 31, New York, NY
June 2, 1970

Robert Arthur Campbell, 25, New York, NY
August 26, 1976

Sandra Patricia Campbell, 45, New York, NY
January 16, 1956

Juan Ortega Campos, 32, New York, NY
November 25, 1968

Sean Thomas Canavan, 39, New York, NY
September 9, 1963

John A. Candela, 42, Glen Ridge, NJ
February 23, 1959

Vincent A. Cangelosi, 30, New York, NY
November 8, 1970

Stephen J. Cangialosi, 40, Middletown, NJ
August 15, 1961

Lisa Bella Cannava, 30, New York, NY
December 22, 1970

Brian Cannizzaro, 30, New York, NY
December 1, 1970

Michael R. Canty, 30, Schenectady, NY
January 20, 1971

Louis Anthony Caporicci, 35, New York, NY
May 29, 1966

Jonathan N. Cappello, 23, Garden City, NY
September 29, 1977

James Christopher Cappers, 33, Wading River, NY
August 22, 1968

Richard Michael Caproni, 34, Lynbrook, NY
February 9, 1967

José Manuel Cardona, 32, New York, NY
December 12, 1966

Dennis M Carey, 51, Wantagh, NY
May 23, 1950

Edward Carlino, 46, New York, NY
May 3, 1955

Michael Scott Carlo, 34, New York, NY
May 20, 1967

David G. Carlone, 46, Randolph, NJ
December 17, 1954

Rosemarie C. Carlson, 40, New York, NY
March 14, 1961

Mark Stephen Carney, 41, Rahway, NJ
July 14, 1960

Joyce Ann Carpeneto, 40, New York, NY
October 1, 1960

Jeremy Caz Carrington, 34, New York, NY
May 8, 1967

Michael T. Carroll, 39, New York, NY
May 14, 1962

Peter J. Carroll, 42, New York, NY
May 4, 1959

James Joseph Carson, 32, Massapequa, NY
January 1, 1969

James Marcel Cartier, 26, New York, NY
June 22, 1975

Vivian Casalduc, 45, New York, NY
June 2, 1956

John Francis Casazza, 38, Colts Neck, NJ
July 31, 1963

Paul Regan Cascio, 23, Manhasset, NY
December 23, 1977

Kathleen Anne Hunt-Casey, 43, Middletown, NJ
September 2, 1958

Thomas Anthony Casoria, 29, New York, NY
February 23, 1972

William Otto Caspar, 57, Eatontown, NJ
September 5, 1944

Alejandro Castaño, 35, Englewood, NJ
January 28, 1967

Arcelia Castillo, 49, Elizabeth, NJ
October 22, 1951

Leonard M. Castrianno, 30, New York, NY
February 9, 1971

José Ramón Castro, 37, New York, NY
January 9, 1964

Richard G. Catarelli, 47, New York, NY
May 18, 1954

Christopher Sean Caton, 34, New York, NY
November 27, 1966

Robert John Caufield, 48, Valley Stream, NY
June 5, 1952

Mary Teresa Caulfield, 58, New York, NY
February 16, 1943

Judson Cavalier, 26, Huntington, NY
July 18, 1975

Michael Joseph Cawley, 32, Bellmore, NY
April 6, 1969

Jason David Cayne, 32, Morganville, NJ
November 1, 1968

Juan Armando Ceballos, 47, New York, NY
April 15, 1954

Marcia G. Cecil-Carter, 34, New York, NY
April 21, 1967

Jason Michael Cefalu, 30, West Hempstead, NY
August 13, 1971

Thomas Joseph Celic, 43, New York, NY
April 4, 1958

Ana Mercedes Centeno, 38, Bayonne, NJ
December 4, 1962

Joni Cesta, 37, Bellmore, NY
October 29, 1963

Jeffrey Marc Chairnoff, 35, West Windsor, NJ
September 3, 1966

Swarna Chalasani, 33, Jersey City, NJ
December 30, 1967

William A. Chalcoff, 41, Roslyn, NY
May 14, 1960

Eli Chalouh, 23, New York, NY
July 3, 1978

Charles Lawrence Chan, 23, New York, NY
September 27, 1977

Mandy Chang, 40, New York, NY
February 27, 1961

Mark Lawrence Charette, 38, Millburn, NJ
February 19, 1963

Gregorio Manuel Chavez, 48, New York, NY
December 24, 1952

Jayceryll Malabuyoc de Chavez, 24, Carteret, NJ
February 1, 1977

Pedro Francisco Checo, 35, New York, NY
February 5, 1966

Douglas MacMillan Cherry, 38, Maplewood, NJ
April 2, 1963

Stephen Patrick Cherry, 41, Stamford, CT
September 25, 1959

Vernon Paul Cherry, 49, New York, NY
October 10, 1951

Nestor Julio Chevalier, 30, New York, NY
August 23, 1971

Swede Joseph Chevalier, 26, Locust, NJ
June 3, 1975

Alexander H. Chiang, 51, New City, NY
November 19, 1949

Dorothy J. Chiarchiaro, 61, Glenwood, NJ
October 4, 1939

Luis Alfonso Chimbo, 39, New York, NY
June 7, 1962

Robert Chin, 33, New York, NY
June 30, 1968

Eddie Wing Wai Ching, 29, Union, NJ
July 17, 1972

Nicholas Paul Chiofalo, 39, Selden, NY
September 22, 1961

John G. Chipura, 39, New York, NY
November 27, 1961

Peter A. Chirchirillo, 47, Langhorne, PA
February 7, 1954

Catherine Ellen Chirls, 47, Princeton, NJ
August 31, 1954

Kyung Hee Casey Cho, 30, Clifton, NJ
May 20, 1971

Abul K. Chowdhury, 30, New York, NY
February 1, 1971

Mohammed Salahuddin Chowdhury, 38, New York, NY
September 15, 1962

Kirsten Lail Christophe, 39, Maplewood, NJ
November 20, 1961

Pamela Chu, 31, New York, NY
February 2, 1970

Steven Paul Chucknick, 44, Cliffwood Beach, NJ
September 8, 1957

Wai-Ching Chung, 36, New York, NY
April 30, 1965

Christopher Ciafardini, 30, New York, NY
May 8, 1971

Alex F. Ciccone, 38, New Rochelle, NY
July 24, 1963

Frances Ann Cilente, 26, New York, NY
November 16, 1974

Elaine Cillo, 40, New York, NY
October 31, 1960

Edna Cintron, 46, New York, NY
October 14, 1954

Nestor Andre Cintron, 26, New York, NY
November 2, 1974

Lt. Robert Dominick Cirri, 39, Nutley, NJ
August 31, 1962

Juan Pablo Cisneros, 23, Weehawken, NJ
December 6, 1977

Benjamin Keefe Clark, 39, New York, NY
June 30, 1962

Eugene Clark, 47, New York, NY
May 18, 1954

Gregory Alan Clark, 40, Teaneck, NJ
September 23, 1960

Mannie Leroy Clark, 54, New York, NY
May 16, 1947

Thomas R. Clark, 37, Summit, NJ
December 13, 1963

Christopher Robert Clarke, 34, Philadelphia, PA
July 8, 1967

Donna Marie Clarke, 39, New York, NY
October 31, 1961

Michael J. Clarke, 27, Prince's Bay, NY
January 11, 1974

Suria Rachel Emma Clarke, 30, New York, NY
August 27, 1971

Kevin Francis Cleary, 38, New York, NY
April 16, 1963

James D. Cleere, 55, Newton, IA
May 13, 1946

Geoffrey W. Cloud, 36, Stamford, CT
August 3, 1965

Susan Marie Clyne, 42, Lindenhurst, NY
May 9, 1959

Steven Coakley, 36, Deer Park, NY
October 25, 1964

Jeffrey Alan Coale, 31, Souderton, PA
July 17, 1970

Patricia A. Cody, 46, Brigantine, NJ
August 25, 1955

Daniel Michael Coffey, 54, Newburgh, NY
April 20, 1947

Jason Matthew Coffey, 25, Newburgh, NY
December 20, 1975

Florence G. Cohen, 62, New York, NY
July 8, 1939

Kevin Sanford Cohen, 28, Edison, NJ
July 2, 1973

Anthony Joseph Coladonato, 47, New York, NY
January 6, 1954

Mark Joseph Colaio, 34, New York, NY
March 2, 1967

Stephen J. Colaio, 32, Montauk, NY
March 30, 1969

Christopher Michael Colasanti, 33, Hoboken, NJ
January 6, 1968

Kevin Nathaniel Colbert, 25, New York, NY
August 26, 1976

Michel P. Colbert, 39, West New York, NJ
January 30, 1962

Keith Eugene Coleman, 34, Warren, NJ
August 15, 1967

Scott Thomas Coleman, 31, New York, NY
June 3, 1970

Tarel Coleman, 32, New York, NY
August 30, 1969

Liam Joseph Colhoun, 34, Flushing,, NY
December 1, 1966

Robert D. Colin, 49, West Babylon, NY
March 31, 1952

Robert J. Coll, 35, Glen Ridge, NJ
December 29, 1965

Jean Marie Collin, 42, New York, NY
November 3, 1958

John Michael Collins, 42, New York, NY
October 21, 1958

Michael L. Collins, 38, Montclair, NJ
October 9, 1962

Thomas Joseph Collins, 36, New York, NY
July 8, 1965

Joseph Kent Collison, 50, New York, NY
May 20, 1951

Patricia Malia Colodner, 39, New York, NY
December 12, 1961

Linda M. Colon, 46, Perrineville, NJ
October 27, 1954

Sol E. Colon, 39, New York, NY
August 19, 1962

Ronald Comer, 56, Northport, NY
October 10, 1944

Jaime Concepcion, 46, New York, NY
November 15, 1954

Albert Conde, 62, Englishtown, NJ
May 29, 1939

Denease Conley, 44, New York, NY
May 28, 1957

Susan P. Conlon, 41, New York, NY
April 11, 1960

Margaret Mary Conner, 57, New York, NY
August 27, 1947

Cynthia Marie L. Connolly, 40, Metuchen, NJ
August 9, 1961

John E. Connolly, 46, Allenwood, NJ
December 24, 1954

James Lee Connor, 38, Summit, NJ
July 22, 1963

Jonathan M. Connors, 55, Old Brookville, NY
April 20,. 1946

Kevin Patrick Connors, 55, Greenwich, CT
July 26, 1946

Kevin Francis Conroy, 47, New York, NY
January 4, 1954

Brenda E. Conway, 40, New York, NY
February 19, 1961

Dennis Michael Cook, 33, Colts Neck, NJ
April 27, 1968

Helen D. Cook, 24, New York, NY
December 29, 1976

John A. Cooper, 40, Bayonne, NJ
June 5, 1961

Joseph John Coppo, 47, New Canaan, CT
December 10, 1953

Gerard J. Coppola, 46, New Providence, NJ
November 12, 1954

Joseph Albert Corbett, 28, Islip, NY
November 15, 1972

Alejandro Cordero, 23, New York, NY
November 26, 1977

Robert Joseph Cordice, 28, New York, NY
October 17, 1972

Ruben D. Correa, 44, New York, NY
January 13, 1957

Danny A. Correa-Gutierrez, 25, Fairview, NJ
March 5, 1976

James Corrigan, 60, New York, NY
February 21, 1941

Carlos Cortés-Rodríguez, 57, New York, NY
September 29, 1943

Kevin M. Cosgrove, 46, West Islip, NY
January 6, 1955

Dolores Marie Costa, 53, Middletown, NJ
September 13, 1948

Digna Alexandra Rivera Costanza, 25, New York, NY
June 13, 1976

Charles Gregory Costello, 46, Old Bridge, NJ
February 24, 1955

Michael S. Costello, 27, Hoboken, NJ
September 6, 1974

Conrod Kofi Cottoy, 51, New York, NY
November 3, 1950

Martin Coughlan, 54, New York, NY
July 1, 1948

Sgt. John Gerard Coughlin, 43, Pomona, NY
November 17, 1957

Timothy John Coughlin, 42, New York, NY
November 15, 1958

James E. Cove, 48, Rockville Centre, NY
September 27, 1952

Andre Colin Cox, 29, New York, NY
May 11, 1972

Frederick John Cox, 27, New York, NY
August 1, 1974

James Raymond Coyle, 26, New York, NY
May 5, 1975

Michelle Coyle-Eulau, 38, Garden City, NY
March 27, 1963

Anne M. Martino-Cramer, 47, New York, NY
March 30, 1954

Christopher Seton Cramer, 34, Manahawkin, NJ
December 24, 1966 ·

Denise Elizabeth Crant, 46, Hackensack, NJ
December 15, 1954

James L. Crawford, 33, Madison, NJ
July 28, 1968

Robert James Crawford, 62, New York, NY
April 1, 1939

Joanne Mary Cregan, 32, New York, NY
July 14, 1969

Lucia Crifasi, 51, Glendale, NY
May 27, 1950

Lt. John A. Crisci, 48, Holbrook, NY
May 25, 1953

Daniel Hal Crisman, 25, New York, NY
June 11, 1976

Dennis A. Cross, 60, Islip Terrace, NY
April 26, 1941

Helen Crossin-Kittle, 34, Larchmont, NY
July 3, 1967

Kevin Raymond Crotty, 43, Summit, NJ
February 10, 1958

Thomas G. Crotty, 42, Rockville Centre, NY
June 5, 1959

John R. Crowe, 57, Rutherford, NJ
March 17, 1944

Welles Remy Crowther, 24, Upper Nyack, NY
May 17, 1977

Robert L. Cruikshank, 64, New York, NY
October 5, 1936

Francisco Cruz Cubero, 47, New York, NY
April 2, 1954

John Robert Cruz, 32, Jersey City, NJ
December 26, 1968

Kenneth John Cubas, 48, Woodstock, NY
February 15, 1953

Richard Joseph Cudina, 46, Glen Gardner, NJ
August 26, 1955

Neil James Cudmore, 38, Port Washington, NY
February 28, 1962

Thomas Patrick Cullen, 31, New York, NY
August 9, 1970

Joan McConnell Cullinan, 47, Scarsdale, NY
August 12, 1954

Joyce Rose Cummings, 65, New York, NY
June 17, 1936

Brian Thomas Cummins, 38, Manasquan, NJ
January 6, 1963

Michael Joseph Cunningham, 39, Princeton Junction, NJ
December 24, 1961

Robert Curatolo, 31, New York, NY
March 2, 1970

Laurence Damian Curia, 41, Garden City, NY
September 15, 1959

Paul Dario Curioli, 53, Norwalk, CT
October 22, 1948

Beverly L. Curry, 41, New York, NY
June 24, 1960

Sgt. Michael Sean Curtin, 45, Medford, NY
August 24, 1956

Gavin Cushny, 47, Hoboken, NJ
November 15, 1953

D

Caleb Arron Dack, 39, Montclair, NJ
December 22, 1962

Carlos S. da Costa, 41, Elizabeth, NJ
April 11, 1960

John D'Allara, 47, Pearl River, NY
August 26, 1954

Vincent Gerard D'Amadeo, 36, East Patchogue, NY
November 25, 1964

Thomas A. Damaskinos, 33, Matawan, NJ
April 17, 1968

Jack L. D'Ambrosi, 45, Woodcliff Lake, NJ
May 25, 1956

Jeannine Marie Damiani-Jones, 28, New York, NY
October 7, 1972

Manuel João DaMota, 43, Valley Stream, NY
November 26, 1957

Patrick W. Danahy, 35, Yorktown Heights, NY
February 21, 1966

Mary D'Antonio, 55, New York, NY
December 26, 1945

Vincent G. Danz, 38, Farmingdale, NY
February 26, 1963

Dwight Donald Darcy, 55, Bronxville, NY
January 21, 1946

Elizabeth Ann Darling, 28, Newark, NJ
August 8, 1973

Annette Andrea Dataram, 25, New York, NY
January 20, 1976

Lt. Edward Alexander D'Atri, 38, New York, NY
February 25, 1963

Michael D. D'Auria, 25, New York, NY
February 16, 1976

Lawrence Davidson, 51, New York, NY
January 31, 1950

Michael Allen Davidson, 27, Westfield, NJ
June 7, 1974

Scott Matthew Davidson, 33, New York, NY
January 4, 1968

Titus Davidson, 55, New York, NY
November 20, 1949

Niurka Davila, 47, New York, NY
April 12, 1954

Clinton Davis, 38, New York, NY
November 12, 1962

Wayne Terrial Davis, 29, Fort Meade, MD
October 1, 1971

Calvin Dawson, 46, New York, NY
March 2, 1955

Anthony Richard Dawson, 32, Southampton,
   Hampshire, England
August 7, 1969

Edward James Day, 45, New York, NY
October 31, 1955

William Thomas Dean, 35, Floral Park, NY
February 8, 1966

Robert J. DeAngelis, 48, West Hempstead, NY
January 8, 1954

Thomas Patrick DeAngelis, 51, Westbury, NY
April 27, 1950

Tara E. Debek, 35, Babylon, NY
August 15, 1965

Anna M. DeBin, 30, East Farmingdale, NY
June 19, 1971

James V. DeBlase, 45, Manalapan, NJ
June 26, 1956

Paul DeCola, 39, Ridgewood, NY
May 28, 1962

Simon Marash Dedvukaj, 26, Mohegan Lake, NY
February 17, 1975

Jason Christopher DeFazio, 29, New York, NY
July 12, 1972

David A. DeFeo, 37, New York, NY
October 12, 1964

Monique E. DeJesús, 28, New York, NY
December 26, 1972

Jennifer De Jesús, 23, New York, NY
December 4, 1977

Nereida De Jesús, 30, New York, NY
November 2, 1970

Emerita (Emy) De La Peña, 32, New York, NY
October 6, 1968

Azucena Maria de la Torre, 50, New York, NY
January 8, 1951

Manuel Del Valle, 32, New York, NY
May 25, 1969

Donald Arthur Delapenha, 37, Allendale, NJ
September 24, 1963

Vito Joseph DeLeo, 41, New York, NY
March 23, 1960

Danielle Ann Delie, 47, New York, NY
July 8, 1954

Joseph A. Della Pietra, 24, New York, NY
March 31, 1977

Andrea DellaBella, 59, Jersey City, NJ
May 24, 1942

Palmina DelliGatti, 33, New York, NY
August 30, 1968

Colleen Ann Deloughery, 41, Bayonne, NJ
June 4, 1960

Francis Albert De Martini, 49, New York, NY
March 31, 1952

Anthony Demas, 61, New York, NY
August 4, 1940

Martin DeMeo, 47, Farmingville, NY
June 20, 1954

Francis X. Deming, 47, Franklin Lakes, NJ
August 29, 1954

Carol Keyes Demitz, 49, New York, NY
October 17, 1951

Kevin Dennis, 43, Peapack, NJ
July 13, 1958

Thomas Francis Dennis, 43, Setauket, NY
January 28, 1958

Jean C. DePalma, 42, Newfoundland, NJ
March 28, 1959

José Nicolas De Pena, 42, New York, NY
March 23, 1959

Robert John Deraney, 43, New York, NY
April 20, 1958

Michael DeRienzo, 37, Hoboken, NJ
December 11, 1965

David Paul DeRubbio, 38, New York, NY
March 9, 1963

Jemal Legesse DeSantis, 28, Jersey City, NJ
December 30, 1972

Christian Louis DeSimone, 23, Ringwood, NJ
October 18, 1977

Edward DeSimone III, 36, Atlantic Highlands, NJ
September 15, 1964

Lt. Andrew Desperito, 44, Patchogue, NY
December 28, 1957

Michael Jude D'Esposito, 32, Morganville, NJ
March 27, 1969

Cindy Ann Deuel, 28, New York, NY
December 7, 1972

Melanie Louise de Vere, 30, London, England
March 15, 1971

Jerry DeVito, 66, New York, NY
July 30, 1935

Robert P. Devitt, 36, Plainsboro, NJ
December 28, 1964

Dennis Lawrence Devlin, 51, Washingtonville, NY
July 1, 1950

Gerard P. Dewan, 35, New York, NY
April 16, 1966

Sulemanali Kassamali Dhanani, 62, Hartsdale, NY
November 4, 1938

Michael Louis DiAgostino, 41, Garden City, NY
July 15, 1960

Matthew Diaz, 33, New York, NY
August 3, 1968

Nancy Diaz, 28, New York, NY
August 6, 1973

Obdulio Ruiz Diaz, 44, New York, NY
September 4, 1957

Michael Díaz-Piedra III, 49, Washington Township, NHJ
January 15, 1952

Judith Berquis Diaz-Sierra, 32, Bay Shore, NY
October 4, 1968

Patricia Florence Di Chiaro, 63, New York, NY
March 17, 1938

Joseph Dermot Dickey, 50, Manhasset, NY
February 7, 1951

Lawrence Patrick Dickinson, 35, Morganville, NJ
December 4, 1965

Michael David Diehl, 48, Brick, NJ
October 1, 1952

John Difato, 39, New York, NY
August 31, 1962

Vincent Francis DiFazio, 43, Hampton, NJ
May 21, 1958

Carl Anthony DiFranco, 27, New York, NY
October 31, 1973

Donald J. DiFranco, 43, New York, NY
February 2, 1958

Debra Ann Di Martino, 36, New York, NY
January 18, 1965

Stephen Patrick Dimino, 48, Basking Ridge, NJ
February 9, 1953

William John Dimmling, 47, Garden City, NY
March 10, 1954

Christopher More Dincuff, 31, Jersey City, NJ
November 26, 1969

Jeffrey Mark Dingle, 32, New York, NY
November 21, 1968

Anthony Dionisio, 38, Glen Rock, NJ
July 31, 1963

George DiPasquale, 33, New York, NY
September 23, 1967

Joseph Di Pilato, 57, New York, NY
August 1, 1944

Douglas Frank DiStefano, 24, Hoboken, NJ
June 2, 1977

Ramzi A. Doany, 35, Bayonne, NJ
August 19, 1966

John Joseph Doherty, 58, Hartsdale, NY
February 8, 1943

Melissa Cándida Doi, 32, New York, NY
September 1, 1969

Brendan Dolan, 37, Glen Rock, NJ
January 20, 1964

Neil Matthew Dollard, 28, Hoboken, NJ
April 29, 1973

James Joseph Domanico, 56, New York, NY
March 11, 1945

Benilda Pascua Domingo, 37, New York, NY
September 29, 1963

Carlos Dominguez, 34, East Meadow, NY
November 11, 1966

Jerome Mark Patrick Dominguez, 37, Holtsville, NY
April 25, 1964

Lt. Kevin W. Donnelly, 43, New York, NY
July 11, 1958

Jacqueline Donovan, 34, New York, NY
May 20, 1967

Stephen Scott Dorf, 39, New Milford, NJ
February 25, 1962

Thomas Dowd, 37, Monroe, NY
April 17, 1964

Lt. Kevin Christopher Dowdell, 46, New York, NY
January 7, 1955

Mary Yolanda Dowling, 46, New York, NY
July 22, 1955

Raymond Matthew Downey, 63, Deer Park, NY
September 19, 1937

Joseph Michael Doyle, 25, New York, NY
March 28, 1976

Frank Joseph Doyle, 39, Englewood, NJ
January 29, 1962

Randall L. Drake, 37, Lee's Summit, MO
January 31, 1964

Stephen Patrick Driscoll, 38, Lake Carmel, NY
July 4, 1963

Mirna A. Duarte, 31, New York, NY
December 10, 1970

Luke A. Dudek, 50, Livingston, NJ
November 19, 1950

Christopher Michael Duffy, 23, New York, NY
February 19, 1978

Gerard J. Duffy, 53, Manorville, NY
January 7, 1948

Michael Joseph Duffy, 29, Northport, NY
September 18, 1971

Thomas W. Duffy, 52, Pittsford, NY
April 24, 1949

Antoinette Duger, 44, Belleville, NJ
February 18, 1967

Jackie Sayegh Duggan, 34, New York, NY
July 25, 1967

Sareve Dukat, 53, New York, NY
January 30, 1948

Christopher Joseph Dunne, 28, Mineola, NY
April 6, 1973

Richard Anthony Dunstan, 54, New Providence, NJ
October 11, 1946

Patrick Thomas Dwyer, 37, Nissequogue, NY
March 30, 1964

E

Joseph Anthony Eacobacci, 26, New York, NY
November 4, 1974

John Bruce Eagleson, 53, Middlefield, CT
May 19, 1948

Robert Douglas Eaton, 37, Manhasset, NY
January 12, 1964

Dean Phillip Eberling, 44, Cranford, NJ
May 24, 1957

Margaret Ruth Echtermann, 33, Hoboken, NJ
August 15, 1968

Paul Robert Eckna, 28, West New York, NJ
April 18, 1973

Constantine Economos, 41, New York, NY
January 5, 1960

Dennis Michael Edwards, 35, Huntington, NY
April 28, 1966

Michael Hardy Edwards, 33, New York, NY
March 26, 1968

Christine Egan, 55, Winnipeg, Manitoba, Canada
June 20, 1946

Lisa Erin Egan, 31, Cliffside Park, NJ
June 25, 1970

Capt. Martin J. Egan, 36, New York, NY
December 14, 1964

Michael Egan, 51, Middletown, NJ
July 13, 1950

Samantha Martin Egan, 24, Jersey City, NJ
May 16, 1977

Carole Eggert, 60, New York, NY
September 24, 1940

Lisa Caren Ehrlich, 36, New York, NY
May 10, 1965

John Ernst Eichler, 69, Cedar Grove, NJ
December 22, 1931

Eric Adam Eisenberg, 32, Commack, NY
October 15, 1968

Daphne Ferlinda Elder, 36, Newark, NJ
July 25, 1965

Michael J. Elferis, 27, College Point, NY
October 14, 1973

Mark Joseph Ellis, 26, South Huntington, NY
June 19, 1975

Valerie Silver Ellis, 46, New York, NY
July 4, 1955

Albert Alfy William Elmarry, 30, North Brunswick, NJ
November 4, 1970

Edgar Hendricks Emery, 45, Clifton, NJ
November 5, 1955

Doris Suk-Yuen Eng, 30, New York, NY
August 30, 1971

Christopher S. Epps, 29, New York, NY
August 8, 1972

Ulf Ramm Ericson, 79, Greenwich, CT
July 26, 1922

Erwin L. Erker, 41, Farmingdale, NY
August 7, 1960

William John Erwin, 30, Verona, NJ
October 15, 1970

Sarah Ali Escarcega, 35, New York, NY
February 8, 1966

José Espinal, 31, New York, NY
March 18, 1970

Billy Scoop Esposito, 51, Bellmore, NY
October 6, 1949

Brigette Ann Esposito, 34, New York, NY
April 22, 1968

Fanny Espinoza, 29, Teaneck, NJ
May 9, 1972

Francis Esposito, 32, New York, NY
August 23, 1969

Lt. Michael Esposito, 41, New York, NY
November 19, 1959

Ruben Esquilin, 35, New York, NY
February 23, 1966

Sadie Ette, 36, New York, NY
February 9, 1965

Barbara G. Etzold, 43, Jersey City, NJ
June 1, 1958

Eric Brian Evans, 31, Weehawken, NJ
September 28, 1969

Robert Edward Evans, 36, Franklin Square, NY
April 27, 1965

Meredith Emily June Ewart, 29, Hoboken, NJ
June 25, 1972

F

Catherine K. Fagan, 58, New York, NY
November 20, 1943

Patricia Mary Fagan, 55, Toms River, NJ
July 21, 1946

Keith George Fairben, 24, Floral Park, NY
October 20, 1976

Sandra Fajardo-Smith, 37, New York, NY
March 2, 1964

William F. Fallon, 53, Rocky Hill, NJ
July 30, 1948

William Lawrence Fallon, 38, Coram, NY
September 20, 1962

Anthony J. Fallone, 39, New York, NY
July 13, 1962

Dolores Brigitte Fanelli, 38, Farmingville, NY
May 6, 1963

John Joseph Fanning, 54, West Hempstead, NY
March 6, 1947

Kathleen Anne Faragher, 33, Denver, Colo.
December 4, 1967

Capt. Thomas James Farino, 37, Bohemia, NY
August 30, 1964

Nancy C. Doloszycki Farley, 45, Jersey City, NJ
October 7, 1955

Elizabeth Ann Farmer, 62, New York, NY
October 15, 1938

Douglas Jon Farnum, 33, New York, NY
June 23, 1968

John Gerard Farrell, 32, New York, NY
June 30, 1969

John W. Farrell, 41, Basking Ridge, NJ
January 23, 1960

Terrence Patrick Farrell, 45, Huntington, NY
March 10, 1956

Capt. Joseph D. Farrelly, 47, New York, NY
August 3, 1954

Thomas Patrick Farrelly, 54, East Northport, NY
March 17, 1947

Syed Abdul Fatha, 54, Newark, NJ
February 26, 1947

Christopher Faughnan, 37, South Orange, NJ
October 31, 1963

Wendy R. Faulkner, 47, Mason, OH
July 25, 1954

Shannon Marie Fava, 30, New York, NY
February 12, 1971

Bernard D. Favuzza, 52, Suffern, NY
April 13, 1949

Robert Fazio, 41, Freeport, NY
May 11, 1960

Ronald Carl Fazio, 57, Closter, NJ
January 19, 1944

William M. Feehan, 72, New York, NY
September 29, 1929

Francis J. Jude Feely, 41, Middletown, NY
September 25, 1959

Garth Erin Feeney, 28, New York, NY
April 6, 1976

Sean Bernard Fegan, 34, New York, NY
March 8, 1967

Lee S. Fehling, 28, Wantagh, NY
October 1, 1972

Peter Adam Feidelberg, 34, Hoboken, NJ
April 6, 1967

Alan D. Feinberg, 48, New York, NY
February 28, 1953

Rosa Maria Feliciano, 30, New York, NY
December 20, 1970

Edward Thomas Fergus, 40, Wilton, CT
May 11, 1961

George J. Ferguson, 54, Teaneck, NJ
January 26, 1947

Henry Fernandez, 23, New York, NY
January 10, 1978

Judy Hazel Santillan Fernandez, 27, Parlin, NJ
January 6, 1974

Julio Fernandez, 51, New York, NY
November 18, 1949

Elisa Giselle Ferraina, 27, London, England
October 14, 1974

Anne Marie Sallerin Ferreira, 29, Jersey City, NJ
August 12, 1972

Robert John Ferris, 63, Garden City, NY
July 2, 1938

David Francis Ferrugio, 46, Middletown, NJ
February 11, 1965

Louis V. Fersini, 38, Basking Ridge, NJ
June 24, 1963

Michael David Ferugio, 37, New York, NY
May 25, 1964

Bradley James Fetchet, 24, New York, NY
November 17, 1976

Jennifer Louise Fialko, 29, Teaneck, NJ
October 13, 1971

Kristen Nicole Fiedel, 27, New York, NY
July 6, 1974

Samuel Fields, 36, New York, NY
August 8, 1965

Michael Bradley Finnegan, 37, Basking Ridge, NJ
March 14, 1964

Timothy J. Finnerty, 33, Glen Rock, NJ
July 15, 1968

Michael Curtis Fiore, 46, New York, NY
July 26, 1955

Stephen J. Fiorelli, 43, Aberdeen, NJ
June 9, 1958

Paul M. Fiori, 31, Yorktown Heights, NY
September 29, 1969

John B. Fiorito, 40, Stamford, CT
January 16, 1961

Andrew Fisher, 42, New York, NY
April 17, 1959

Bennett Lawson Fisher, 58, Stamford, CT
November 25, 1942

John Roger Fisher, 46, Bayonne, NJ
February 24, 1955

Thomas J. Fisher, 36, Union, NJ
November 15, 1964

Lucy A. Fishman, 37, New York, NY
December 30, 1964

Ryan D. Fitzgerald, 26, New York, NY
April 30, 1975

Thomas James Fitzpatrick, 35, Tuckahoe, NY
October 24, 1965

Richard P. Fitzsimons, 57, Lynbrook, NY
December 28, 1943

Salvatore A. Fiumefreddo, 47, Manalapan, NJ
March 17, 1956

Christina Donovan Flannery, 26, New York, NY
August 10, 1975

Eileen Flecha, 33, New York, NY
February 19, 1968

Andre G. Fletcher, 37, North Babylon, NY
February 25, 1964

Carl M. Flickinger, 38, Conyers, NY
April 25, 1963

John Joseph Florio, 33, Oceanside, NY
November 29, 1967

Joseph Walkden Flounders, 46, East Stroudsburg, PA
January 31, 1955

David Fodor, 38, Garrison, NY
April 6, 1963

Lt. Michael N. Fodor, 53, Warwick, NY
May 14, 1948

Steven Mark Fogel, 40, Westfield, NY
February 22, 1961

Thomas J. Foley, 32, West Nyack, NY
January 18, 1969

David J. Fontana, 37, New York, NY
October 17, 1963

Chih Min Foo, 40, Holmdel, NJ
October 28, 1960

Delrose E. Forbes Cheatham, 48, New York, NY
September 15, 1952

Godwin Forde, 39, New York, NY
September 30, 1962

Donald A. Foreman, 53, New York, NY
February 4, 1948

Christopher Hugh Forsythe, 44, Basking Ridge, NJ
October 19, 1956

Claudia Alicia Foster, 26, New York, NY
April 28, 1975

Noel John Foster, 40, Bridgewater, NJ
November 4, 1960

Ana Fosteris, 58, Coram, NY
April 1, 1943

Robert Joseph Foti, 42, Albertson, NY
August 19, 1959

Jeffrey L. Fox, 40, Cranbury, NJ
November 14, 1960

Virginia Elizabeth Fox, 58, New York, NY
June 16, 1943

Pauline Francis, 57, New York, NY
December 23, 1944

Virgin Lucy Francis, 62, New York, NY
March 6, 1939

Gary Jay Frank, 35, South Amboy, NJ
November 5, 1965

Morton H. Frank, 31, New York, NY
February 5, 1970

Peter Christopher Frank, 29, New York, NY
December 1, 1971

Richard K. Fraser, 32, New York, NY
November 12, 1968

Kevin J. Frawley, 34, Bronxville, NY
January 29, 1967

Clyde Frazier, 41, New York, NY
February 9, 1960

Lillian Inez Frederick, 46, Teaneck, NJ
December 27, 1954

Andrew Fredericks, 40, Suffern, NY
February 20, 1961

Tamitha Freemen, 35, New York, NY
August 26, 1966

Brett Owen Freiman, 29, Roslyn, NY
October 19, 1972

Lt. Peter L. Freund, 45, Westtown, NY
December 19, 1955

Arlene Eva Fried, 49, Roslyn Heights, NY
April 21, 1952

Alan W. Friedlander, 52, Yorktown Heights, NY
April 23, 1949

Andrew Keith Friedman, 44, Woodbury, NY
March 26, 1957

Gregg J. Froehner, 46, Chester, NJ
March 22, 1955

Peter Christian Fry, 36, Wilton, CT
August 26, 1965

Clement Fumando, 59, New York, NY
February 18, 1942

Steven Elliot Furman, 40, Wesley Hills, NY
September 13, 1960

Paul James Furmato, 37, Colts Neck, NJ
October 3, 1963

G

Fredric Neal Gabler, 30, New York, NY
March 3, 1971

Richard S. Gabrielle, 50, West Haven, CT
December 14, 1950

James Andrew Gadiel, 23, New York, NY
February 3, 1978

Pamela Lee Gaff, 51, Robinsville, NJ
September 10, 1950

Ervin Vincent Gailliard, 42, New York, NY
February 23, 1959

Deanna Lynn Galante and her unborn, 32, New York, NY
August 1, 1969

Grace Catherine Galante, 29, New York, NY
August 2, 1972

Anthony Edward Gallagher, 41, New York, NY
May 31, 1960

Daniel James Gallagher, 23, Red Bank, NJ
July 4, 1978

John Patrick Gallagher, 31, Yonkers, NY
October 14, 1969

Lourdes J. Galletti Diaz, 32, New York, NY
May 21, 1966

Cono E. Gallo, 30, New York, NY
May 2, 1971

Vincent Gallucci, 36, Monroe Township, NJ
October 25, 1964

Thomas Edward Galvin, 32, New York, NY
November 29, 1968

Giovanna Galletta Gambale, 27, New York, NY
July 5, 1974

Thomas Gambino, Jr., 48, Babylon, NY
August 14, 1953

Giann F. Gamboa, 26, New York, NY
November 29, 1974

Peter J. Ganci, Jr., 55, North Massapequa, NY
October 27, 1946

Michael Gann, 41, Roswell, GA
February 14, 1960

Lt. Charles William Garbarini, 44, Westchester, NY
April 22, 1957

Cesar R. Garcia, 36, New York, NY
April 30, 1965

David Garcia, 40, Freeport, NY
May 11, 1961

Jorge Luis Morron Garcia, 38, New York, NY
September 30, 1962

Juan Garcia, 50, New York, NY
January 23, 1951

Marlyn Del Carmen Garcia, 21, New York, NY
March 6, 1980

Christopher Samuel Gardner, 36, Darien, CT
June 9, 1965

Douglas Benjamin Gardner, 39, New York, NY
October 5, 1961

Harvey Joseph Gardner, 35, Lake Wood, NJ
June 20, 1966

Jeffrey Brian Gardner, 36, Hoboken, NJ
June 1, 1965

Thomas A. Gardner, 39, Oceanside, NY
August 1, 1962

William Arthur Gardner, 45, Lynbrook, NY
November 6, 1955

Francesco Garfi, 29, New York, NY
October 20, 1972

Rocco Nino Gargano, 28, Bayside, NY
January 16, 1973

James M. Gartenberg, 36, New York, NY
December 23, 1965

Matthew David Garvey, 37, New York, NY
October 31, 1963

Bruce Gary, 51, Bellmore, NY
July 7, 1950

Boyd Alan Gatton, 38, Jersey City, NJ
October 8, 1962

Donald Richard Gavagan, Jr., 35, New York, NY
July 13, 1966

Terence D. Gazzani, 24, New York, NY
February 23, 1977

Gary Paul Geidel, 44, New York, NY
December 11, 1956

Paul Hamilton Geier, 36, Farmingdale, NY
August 12, 1965

Julie M. Geis, 44, Lees Summit, MO
August 14, 1957

Peter Gerard Gelinas, 34, New York, NY
August 6, 1967

Steven Paul Geller, 52, New York, NY
April 14, 1949

Howard G. Gelling, Jr., 28, New York, NY
August 18, 1973

Peter Victor Genco, Jr., 36, Rockville Centre, NY
October 18, 1964

Steven Gregory Genovese, 37, Basking Ridge, NJ
July 25, 1964

Alayne F. Gentul, 44, Mountain Lakes, NJ
October 4, 1956

Edward F. Geraghty, 45, Rockville Centre, NY
February 10, 1956

Suzanne Geraty, 30, New York, NY
July 26, 1971

Ralph Gerhardt, 33, New York, NY
June 6, 1967

Robert J. Gerlich, 56, Monroe, CT
March 23, 1945

Denis P. Germain, 33, Tuxedo Park, NY
October 19, 1967

Marina Romanovna Gertsberg, 25, New York, NY
February 10, 1976

Susan M. Getzendanner, 57, New York, NY
October 27, 1943

James Gerard Geyer, 41, Rockville Centre, NY
June 4, 1960

Joseph M. Giaccone, 43, Monroe, NJ
April 26, 1958

Lt. Vincent Francis Giammona, 40, Valley Stream, NY
September 11, 1961

Debra Lynn Gibbon, 43, Hackettstown, NJ
November 27, 1957

James A. Giberson, 43, New York, NY
October 10, 1957

Craig Neil Gibson, 37, New York, NY
December 26, 1963

Ronnie Gies, 43, Merrick, NY
August 8, 1958

Andrew Clive Gilbert, 39, Tweksbury, NJ
March 7, 1962

Timothy Paul Gilbert, 35, Lebanon, NJ
February 14, 1966

Paul Stuart Gilbey, 39, Chatham, NJ
July 31, 1962

Paul John Gill, 34, New York, NY
April 11, 1967

Mark Y. Gilles, 33, New York, NY
January 15, 1968

Evan Hunter Gillette, 40, New York, NY
May 5, 1961

Ronald Lawrence Gilligan, 43, Norwalk, CT
May 15, 1958

Sgt. Rodney C. Gillis, 34, New York, NY
September 26, 1967

Laura Gilly, 32, New York, NY
January 31, 1969

Lt. John F. Ginley, 37, Warwick, NY
May 21, 1964

Donna Marie Giordano, 44, Parlin, NJ
February 23, 1957

Jeffrey John Giordano, 46, New York, NY
January 21, 1956

John Giordano, 46, Newburgh, NY
January 17, 1954

Steven A. Giorgetti, 43, Manhasset, NY
September 29, 1957

Martin Giovinazzo, 34, New York, NY
October 5, 1966

Kum-Kum Girolamo, 41, New York, NY
January 8, 1960

Salvatore Gitto, 44, Manalapan, NJ
December 18, 1956

Cynthia Giugliano, 46, Nesconset, NY
December 14, 1954

Mon Gjonbalaj, 65, New York, NY
October 1, 1936

Dianne Gladstone, 55, New York, NY
March 22, 1946

Keith Alexander Glascoe, 38, New York, NY
December 9, 1962

Thomas Irwin Glasser, 40, Summit, NJ
October 18, 1960

Harry Glenn, 38, Piscataway, NJ
December 11, 1962

Barry H. Glick, 55, Wayne, NJ
October 1, 1945

Steven Lawrence Glick, 42, Greenwich, CT
July 22, 1959

John T. Gnazzo, 32, New York, NY
May 24, 1969

William Robert Godshalk, 35, New York, NY
May 4, 1966

Michael Gogliormella, 43, New Providence, NJ
January 16, 1958

Brian F. Goldberg, 26, Union, NJ
October 30, 1974

Jeffrey Grant Goldflam, 48, Melville, NY
May 26, 1953

Michelle Herman Goldstein, 31, New York, NY
August 8, 1970

Monica Goldstein, 25, New York, NY
August 9, 1976

Steven Ian Goldstein, 35, Princeton, NJ
April 10, 1966

Andrew H. Golkin, 30, New York, NY
November 3, 1970

Dennis James Gomes, 40, New York, NY
November 1, 1960

Enrique Antonio Gomez, 42, New York, NY
July 15, 1959

José Bienvenido Gómez, 45, New York, NY
August 3, 1956

Manuel Gomez, Jr., 42, New York, NY
January 11, 1959

Wilder Alfredo Gomez, 38, New York, NY
September 22, 1963

Jenine Gonzalez, 27, New York, NY
September 16, 1973

Mauricio Gonzalez, 27, New York, NY
April 4, 1974

Rosa J. Gonzalez, 32, Jersey City, NJ
January 23, 1969

Calvin Joseph Gooding, 38, Riverside, NY
May 26, 1963

Harry Goody, 50, New York, NY
August 6, 1951

Kiran Kumar Reddy Gopu, 24, Bridgeport, CT
August 29, 1976

Catherine Carmen Gorayeb, 41, New York, NY
February 29, 1960

Kerene Gordon, 43, New York, NY
January 5, 1958

Sebastian Gorki, 27, New York, NY
April 23, 1974

Kieran Joseph Gorman, 35, Yonkers, NY
January 5, 1966

Thomas Edward Gorman, 41, Middlesex, NJ
December 27, 1959

Michael Edward Gould, 29, Hoboken, NJ
July 30, 1972

Yugi Goya, 42, Rye, NY
March 31, 1959

Jon Richard Grabowski, 33, New York, NY
October 17, 1967

Christopher Michael Grady, 39, Cranford, NJ
August 13, 1962

Edwin John Graf III, 48, Rowayton, CT
February 10, 1953

David M. Graifman, 40, New York, NY
February 8, 1961

Gilbert Franco Granados, 51, Hicksville, NY
January 10, 1950

Elvira Granitto, 43, New York, NY
March 1, 1958

Winston Arthur Grant, 59, West Hempstead, NY
October 2, 1941

Christopher S. Gray, 32, Weehawken, NJ
February 4, 1969

James Michael Gray, 34, New York, NY
November 8, 1966

John Michael Grazioso, 41, Middletown, NJ
April 28, 1960

Timothy George Grazioso, 42, Gulf Stream, FL
October 4, 1958

Derrick Arthur Green, 44, New York, NY
October 4, 1956

Wade Brian Green, 42, Westbury, NY
November 6, 1958

Elaine Myra Greenberg, 56, New York, NY
September 6, 1945

Gayle R. Greene, 51, Montville, NJ
April 23, 1950

James Arthur Greenleaf, Jr., 32, New York, NY
February 10, 1969

Eileen Marsha Greenstein, 52, Morris Plains, NJ
July 23, 1949

Elizabeth Martin Gregg, 52, New York, NY
March 25, 1949

Denise Gregory, 39, New York, NY
September 21, 1961

Donald H. Gregory, 62, Ramsey, NJ
July 10, 1939

Florence M. Gregory, 38, New York, NY
December 13, 1962

Pedro Grehan, 35, Hoboken, NJ
December 2, 1965

John Michael Griffin, 38, Waldwick, NJ
May 20, 1963

Tawanna Sherry Griffin, 30, New York, NY
September 4, 1971

Joan D. Griffith, 39, Willingboro, NJ
December 19, 1961

Warren Grifka, 54, New York, NY
March 1, 1947

Ramón B. Grijalvo, 58, Hollis, NY
October 10, 1942

Joseph F. Grillo, 46, New York, NY
August 18, 1955

David Joseph Grimner, 51, Merrick, NY
April 20, 1950

Kenneth George Grouzalis, 56, Lyndhurst, NJ
September 6, 1945

Joseph Grzelak, 52, New York, NY
March 22, 1949

Matthew J. Grzymalski, 34, New Hyde Park, NY
February 21, 1967

Robert Joseph Gschaar, 55, Spring Valley, NY
March 8, 1946

Liming (Michael) Gu, 34, Piscataway, NJ
September 4, 1967

José A. Guadalupe, 37, New York, NY
November 26, 1963

Cindy Yan Zhu Guan, 25, New York, NY
June 28, 1976

Geoffrey E. Guja, 47, Lindenhurst, NY
February 27, 1954

Lt. Joseph P. Gullickson, 37, New York, NY
March 19, 1964

Babita Girjamatie Guman, 33, New York, NY
March 25, 1968

Douglas Brian Gurian, 38, Tenafly, NJ
July 6, 1963

Philip T. Guza, 54, Sea Bright, NJ
October 19, 1946

Barbara Guzzardo, 49, Glendale, NY
February 25, 1952

Peter Mark Gyulavary, 44, Warwick, NY
August 27, 1956

H

Gary Robert Haag, 36, Ossining, NY
August 6, 1965

Andrea Lyn Haberman, 25, Chicago, IL
February 2, 1976

Barbara Mary Habib, 49, New York, NY
November 15, 1951

Philip Haentzler, 49, New York, NY
May 12, 1952

Nizam A. Hafiz, 32, New York, NY
April 21, 1969

Karen Elizabeth Hagerty, 34, New York, NY
June 9, 1967

Steven Michael Hagis, 31, New York, NY
September 18, 1969

Mary Lou Hague, 26, New York, NY
October 7, 1947

David Halderman, 40, New York, NY
August 2, 1961

Maile Rachel Hale, 26, Cambridge, MA
February 14, 1975

Richard B. Hall, 49, Purchase, NY
April 30, 1952

Vaswald George Hall, 50, New York, NY
September 7, 1951

Robert John Halligan, 59, Basking Ridge, NJ
June 11, 1942

Lt. Vincent Gerard Halloran, 43, North Salem, NY
July 31, 1958

James D. Halvorson, 56, Greenwich, CT
January 10, 1945

Mohammad Salman Hamdani, 23, New York, NY
December 28, 1977

Felicia Hamilton, 62, New York, NY
June 20, 1939

Robert W. Hamilton, 43, Washingtonville, NY
January 16, 1958

Frederic Kim Han, 45, Marlboro, NJ
March 4, 1956

Christopher James Hanley, 34, New York, NY
September 20, 1966

Sean S. Hanley, 35, New York, NY
June 18, 1966

Valerie Joan Hanna, 57, Freeville, NY
September 6, 1944

Thomas Paul Hannafin, 36, New York, NY
April 20, 1965

Kevin James Hannaford, 32, Basking Ridge, NJ
October 8, 1968

Dana Rey Hannon, 29, Suffern, NY
March 5, 1972

Michael Lawrence Hannan, 34, Lynbrook, NY
January 10, 1967

Vassilios G. Haramis, 56, New York, NY
May 15, 1945

James A. Haran, 41, Malverne, NY
November 12, 1959

Jeffrey Pike Hardy, 46, New York, NY
March 31, 1955

Timothy John (T.J.) Hargrave, 38, Readington, NJ
September 28, 1962

Daniel Edward Harlin, 41, Kent, NY
December 21, 1959

Frances Haros, 76, New York, NY
March 28, 1925

Lt. Harvey L. Harrell, 49, New York, NY
May 3, 1952

Lt. Stephen Gary Harrell, 44, Warwick, NY
April 18, 1957

Melissa Harrington-Hughes, 31, San Francisco, CA
May 29, 1970

Aisha Ann Harris, 22, New York, NY
July 2, 1979

Stewart D. Harris, 52, Marlboro, NJ
June 26, 1949

John Patrick Hart, 38, Danville, CA
February 27, 1963

John Clinton Hartz, 64, Basking Ridge, NJ
February 21, 1937

Emeric J. Harvey, 56, Montclair, NJ
December 4, 1944

Capt. Thomas Theodore Haskell, 37, Massapequa, NY
March 12, 1964

Timothy Shawn Haskell, 34, Seaford, NY
February 25, 1967

Joseph John Hasson, 34, New York, NY
March 2, 1967

Leonard W. Hatton, 45, Ridgefield Park, NJ
August 17, 1956

Capt. Terence S. Hatton, 41, New York, NY
September 26, 1959

Michael Helmut Haub, 34, Roslyn Heights, NY
June 13, 1967

Timothy Aaron Haviland, 41, Oceanside, NY
February 25, 1960

Donald G. Havlish, 53, Yardley, PA
January 25, 1948

Anthony Maurice Hawkins, 30, New York, NY
August 7, 1971

Nobuhiro Hayatsu, 36, Scarsdale, NY
March 7, 1965

Philip T. Hayes, 67, Northport, NY
March 3, 1934

W. Ward Haynes, 35, Rye, NY
December 26, 1965

Scott Jordan Hazelcorn, 29, Hoboken, NJ
August 14, 1972

Lt. Michael K. Healey, 42, East Patchogue, NY
January 7, 1959

Roberta Bernstein Heber, 60, New York, NY
April 8, 1941

Charles Francis Xavier Heeran, 23, Belle Harbor, NY
November 26, 1977

John F. Heffernan, 37, New York, NY
May 26, 1964

H. Joseph Heller, 37, Ridgefield, CT
May 5, 1964

JoAnn L. Heltibridle, 46, Springfield, NJ
July 26, 1955

Mark F. Hemschoot, 45, Red Bank, NJ
August 7, 1956

Ronnie Lee Henderson, 52, Newburgh, NY
July 23, 1949

Brian Hennessey, 35, Ringoes, NJ
September 6, 1966

Michelle Marie Henrique, 27, New York, NY
December 13, 1973

Joseph Patrick Henry, 25, New York, NY
May 24, 1976

William L. Henry, 49, New York, NY
April 29, 1952

John Christopher Henwood, 35, New York, NY
February 15, 1966

Robert Allan Hepburn, 39, Union, NJ
August 17, 1962

Mary Herencia, 47, New York, NY
September 19, 1953

Lindsay Coates Herkness, 58, New York, NY
April 8, 1943

Harvey Robert Hermer, 59, New York, NY
May 6, 1942

Claribel Villalobos Hernandez, 31, New York, NY
September 6, 1970

Norberto Hernandez, 42, New York, NY
March 9, 1959

Raul Hernandez, 51, New York, NY
October 12, 1949

Gary Herold, 44, Farmingdale, NY
December 20, 1956

Jeffrey Alan Hersch, 53, New York, NY
April 4, 1948

Thomas J. Hetzel, 33, Elmont, NY
December 23, 1967

Capt. Brian Christopher Hickey, 47, New York, NY
June 11, 1954

Lt. Timothy Brian Higgins, 43, Farmingville, NY
March 2, 1958

Robert D. W. Higley, 29, New Fairfield, CT
November 22, 1971

Todd Russell Hill, 34, Boston, MA
February 3, 1967

Clara Victorine Hinds, 52, New York, NY
November 26, 1948

Neal O. Hinds, 28, New York, NY
September 13, 1972

Mark D. Hindy, 28, New York, NY
July 20, 1973

Katsuyuki Hirai, 32, Hartsdale, NY
November 26, 1968

Heather Malia Ho, 32, New York, NY
August 1, 1969

Tara Yvette Hobbs, 31, New York, NY
May 3, 1970

Thomas Anderson Hobbs, 41, Baldwin, NY
December 22, 1959

James J. Hobin, 47, Marlborough, CT
March 18, 1954

Robert Wayne Hobson, 36, New Providence, NJ
October 23, 1964

Bradley Hodges Vadas, 37, Westport, CT
February 29, 1964

DaJuan Hodges, 29, New York, NY
February 26, 1972

Ronald George Hoerner, 58, Massapequa Park, NY
August 30, 1943

Patrick A. Hoey, 53, Middletown, NJ
November 24, 1947

Marcia Hoffman, 52, New York, NY
April 1, 1949

Stephen Gerard Hoffman, 36, Long Beach, NY
December 20, 1964

Frederick Joseph Hoffmann, 53, Freehold, NJ
July 5, 1948

Michele L. Hoffmann, 27, Freehold, NJ
February 21, 1974

Judith Florence Hofmiller, 53, Brookfield, CT
March 21, 1948

Thomas Warren Hohlweck, 57, Harrison, NY
December 25, 1944

Jonathan R. Hohmann, 48, New York, NY
September 4, 1953

John Holland, 30, New York, NY
January 9, 1971

Joseph Francis Holland, 32, Glen Rock, NJ
November 15, 1968

Elizabeth Holmes, 42, New York, NY
August 29, 1958

Thomas P. Holohan, 36, Chester, NY
January 5, 1965

Bradley V. Hoorn, 22, New York, NY
June 3, 1979

James P. Hopper, 51, Farmingdale, NY
January 6, 1949

Montgomery McCullough Hord, 46, Pelham, NY
August 24, 1955

Michael Joseph Horn, 27, Lynbrook, NY
December 27, 1973

Matthew Douglas Horning, 26, Hoboken, NJ
January 16, 1975

Robert L. Horohoe, 31, New York, NY
June 11, 1970

Aaron Horwitz, 24, New York, NY
November 15, 1976

Charles J. Houston, 42, New York, NY
October 18, 1958

Uhuru G. Houston, 32, Englewood, NJ
August 22, 1969

George Gerard Howard, 45, Hicksville, NY
March 11, 1957

Michael C. Howell, 60, New York, NY
November 2, 1940

Steven Leon Howell, 36, New York, NY
August 31, 1965

Jennifer L. Howley, 34, New Hyde Park, NY
July 7, 1967

Milagros "Millie" Hromada, 35, New York, NY
November 27, 1965

Marian Hrycak, 56, New York, NY
February 10, 1945

Stephen Huczko, 44, Bethlehem, NJ
December 15, 1956

Kris Robert Hughes, 30, Nesconset, NY
July 19, 1971

Thomas F. Hughes, 46, Spring Lake Heights, NJ
March 29, 1955

Timothy Robert Hughes, 43, Madison, NJ
September 3, 1958

Paul Rexford Hughes, 38, Stamford, CT
September 14, 1962

Robert T. Hughes, 23, Sayreville, NJ
May 30, 1978

Susan Huie, 43, Fair Lawn, NJ
April 24, 1958

Lamar Demetrius Hulse, 30, New York, NY
June 10, 1971

William Christopher Hunt, 32, Norwalk, CT
July 27, 1969

Joseph Gerard Hunter, 31, South Hempstead, NY
September 29, 1969

Robert R. Hussa, 51, Roslyn, NY
July 31, 1950

Capt. Walter G. Hynes, 46, Belle Harbor, NY
October 2, 1954

Thomas Edward Hynes, 28, Norwalk, CT
December 19, 1972

I

Joseph Anthony Ianelli, 28, Hoboken, NJ
July 6, 1973

Zuhtu Ibis, 25, Clifton, NJ
October 23, 1975

Jonathan Lee Ielpi, 29, Great Neck, NY
July 15, 1972

Michael Patrick Iken, 37, New York, NY
September 8, 1964

Daniel Ilkanayev, 36, New York, NY
December 22, 1964

Capt. Frederick Ill, 49, Pearl River, NY
January 26, 1952

Abraham Nethanel Ilowitz, 51, New York, NY
April 24, 1950

Anthony P. Infante, 47, Chatham, NJ
July 7, 1954

Louis S. Inghilterra, 45, New Castle, NY
December 21, 1955

Christopher N. Ingrassia, 28, Watchung, NJ
April 24, 1973

Paul Innella, 33, East Brunswick, NJ
November 11, 1967

Stephanie V. Irby, 38, New York, NY
December 2, 1962

Douglas Irgang, 32, New York, NY
June 2, 1969

Todd A. Isaac, 29, New York, NY
July 18, 1972

Erik Hans Isbrandtsen, 30, New York, NY
August 2, 1971

Taizo Ishikawa, 50, New York, NY
October 14, 1950

Aram Iskenderian, 41, Merrick, NY
June 6, 1960

John Iskyan, 41, Wilton, CT
April 11, 1960

Kazushige Ito, 35, New York, NY
November 19, 1965

Aleksandr Valeryerich Ivantsov, 23, New York, NY
April 25, 1978

J

Virginia May Jablonski, 49, Matawan, NJ
October 27, 1951

Brooke Alexandra Jackman, 23, New York, NY
August 28, 1978

Aaron Jeremy Jacobs, 27, New York, NY
May 23, 1974

Ariel Louis Jacobs, 29, Briarcliff Manor, NY
September 17, 1971

Jason Kyle Jacobs, 32, Mendham, NJ
November 24, 1968

Michael G. Jacobs, 54, Danbury, CT
November 11, 1946

Steven A. Jacobson, 53, New York, NY
May 25, 1948

Ricknauth Jaggernauth, 58, New York, NY
June 18, 1943

Jake Denis Jagoda, 24, Huntington, NY
July 29, 1977

Yudhvir S. Jain, 54, New City, NY
August 29, 1947

Maria Jakubiak, 41, Ridgewood, NY
May 31, 1961

Ernest James, 40, New York, NY
August 5, 1961

Gricelda E. James, 44, Willingboro, NJ
May 10, 1957

Mark Steven Jardim, 39, New York, NY
June 11, 1962

Muhammadou Jawara, 30, New York, NY
July 20, 1971

François Jean-Pierre, 58, New York, NY
February 6, 1943

Maxima Jean-Pierre, 40, Bellport, NY
October 6, 1960

Paul Edward Jeffers, 39, New York, NY
November 30, 1961

Joseph Jenkins, 47, New York, NY
June 12, 1954

Alan Keith Jensen, 49, Wyckoff, NJ
March 19, 1952

Prem Nath Jerath, 57, Edison, NJ
September 1, 1944

Farah Jeudy, 32, Spring Valley, NY
June 11, 1969

Hweidar Jian, 42, East Brunswick, NJ
February 26, 1959

Eliezer Jimenez, 38, New York, NY
February 9, 1963

Luis Jimenez, 25, New York, NY
November 17, 1975

Charles Gregory John, 44, New York, NY
January 28, 1957

Nicholas John, 42, New York, NY
July 2, 1959

LaShawana Johnson, 27, New York, NY
November 24, 1973

Scott Michael Johnson, 26, New York, NY
April 7, 1975

William R. Johnston, 31, North Babylon, NY
December 1, 1969

Allison Horstmann Jones, 31, New York, NY
July 23, 1970

Arthur Joseph Jones, 37, Ossining, NY
June 25, 1964

Brian Leander Jones, 44, New York, NY
May 9, 1957

Christopher D. Jones, 53, Huntington, NY
September 14, 1947

Donald T. Jones, 39, Livingston, NJ
November 4, 1961

Donald W. Jones, 43, Fairless Hills, PA
August 27, 1958

Linda Jones, 50, New York, NY
February 7, 1951

Mary S. Jones, 72, New York, NY
January 27, 1929

Andrew Brian Jordan, 35, Remsenburg, NY
January 26, 1965

Robert Thomas Jordan, 34, Williston, NY
March 16, 1967

Albert Gunnis Joseph, 79, New York, NY
January 7, 1922

Ingeborg Joseph, 60, Berlin, Germany
October 16, 1940

Karl Henri Joseph, 25, New York, NY
November 5, 1975

Stephen Joseph, 39, Franklin Park, NJ
July 20, 1962

Jane Eileen Josiah, 47, Bellmore, NY
October 17, 1953

Lt. Anthony Jovic, 39, Massapequa, NY
June 4, 1962

Angel L. Juarbe, 35, New York, NY
May 1, 1966

Karen Sue Juday, 52, New York, NY
February 22, 1949

The Rev. Mychal F. Judge, 68, New York, NY
May 11, 1933

Paul William Jurgens, 47, Levittown, NY
July 15, 1954

Thomas Edward Jurgens, 26, Lawrence, NY
November 30, 1974

K

Shashi Lakshmikantha Kadaba, 25, Bangalore, India
January 13, 1975

Gavkharoy Mukhometovna Kamardinova, 26, New York, NY
July 24, 1975

Shari Kandell, 27, Wyckoff, NJ
September 21, 1973

Howard Lee Kane, 40, Hazlet, NJ
May 6, 1961

Jennifer Lynn Kane, 26, Fairlawn, NJ
March 12, 1975

Vincent D. Kane, 37, New York, NY
April 12, 1964

Joon Koo Kang, 34, Riverdale, NJ
January 1, 1967

Sheldon Robert Kanter, 53, Edison, NJ
July 27, 1948

Deborah H. Kaplan, 45, Paramus, NJ
December 28, 1955

Alvin Peter Kappelmann, 57, Green Brook, NJ
August 26, 1944

Charles H. Karczewski, 34, Union, NJ
April 27, 1967

William A. Karnes, 37, New York, NY
March 23, 1964

Douglas G. Karpiloff, 53, Mamaroneck, NY
July 28, 1948

Charles L. Kasper, 54, New York, NY
October 27, 1946

Andrew K. Kates, 37, New York, NY
November 16, 1963

John A. Katsimatides, 31, New York, NY
September 5, 1970

Sgt. Robert Michael Kaulfers, 49, Kenilworth, NJ
July 20, 1952

Don Jerome Kauth, Jr., 51, Saratoga Springs, NY
June 28, 1950

Hideya Kawauchi, 36, Fort Lee, NJ
September 26, 1964

Edward T. Keane, 66, West Caldwell, NJ
June 10, 1935

Richard M. Keane, 54, Wethersfield, CT
July 12, 1947

Lisa Yvonne Kearney-Griffin, 35, Jamaica, NY
June 13, 1966

Karol Ann Keasler, 42, New York, NY
April 21, 1959

Paul Hanlon Keating, 38, New York, NY
September 4, 1963

Leo Russell Keene, III, 33, Westfield, NJ
November 13, 1967

Joseph John Keller, 31, Park Ridge, NJ
January 2, 1970

Peter Rodney Kellerman, 35, New York, NY
February 1, 1966

Joseph P. Kellett, 37, Riverdale, NY
August 12, 1964

Frederick H. Kelley, III, 57, Huntington, NY
July 26, 1944

James Joseph Kelly, 39, Oceanside, NY
November 18, 1961

Joseph A. Kelly, 40, Oyster Bay, NY
November 28, 1960

Maurice Patrick Kelly, 41, New York, NY
January 17, 1960

Richard John Kelly, Jr., 50, New York, NY
August 1, 1951

Thomas Michael Kelly, 41, Wyckoff, NJ
May 11, 1960

Thomas Richard Kelly, 38, Riverhead, NY
February 13, 1962

Thomas W. Kelly, 51, New York, NY
September 18, 1950

Timothy Colin Kelly, 37, Port Washington, NY
December 9, 1963

William Hill Kelly, Jr., 30, New York, NY
January 22, 1971

Robert Clinton Kennedy, 55, Toms River, NJ
December 11, 1945

Thomas J. Kennedy, 36, Islip Terrace, NY
January 24, 1965

John Richard Keohane, 41, Jersey City, NJ
July 16, 1960

Lt. Ronald T. Kerwin, 42, Levittown, NY
October 6, 1958

Howard L. Kestenbaum, 56, Montclair, NJ
December 30, 1944

Douglas D. Ketcham, 27, New York, NY
August 22, 1974

Ruth Ellen Ketler, 42, New York, NY
October 31, 1958

Boris Khalif, 30, New York, NY
April 22, 1971

Sarah Khan, 32, New York, NY
August 24, 1969

Taimour Firaz Khan, 29, New York, NY
December 15, 1971

Rajesh Khandelwal, 33, South Plainfield, NJ
January 12, 1968

SeiLai Khoo, 38, Jersey City, NJ
June 14, 1963

Michael Vernon Kiefer, 25, Franklin Square, NY
December 5, 1975

Satoshi Kikuchihara, 43, Scarsdale, NY
April 14, 1958

Andrew Jay-Hoon Kim, 26, Leonia, NJ
November 25, 1974

Lawrence Don Kim, 31, Blue Bell, PA
November 22, 1969

Mary Jo Kimelman, 34, New York, NY
October 25, 1966

Andrew M. King, 42, Princeton, NJ
August 25, 1959

Lucille Teresa King, 59, Ridgewood, NJ
May 11, 1942

Robert King, Jr., 36, Bellerose Terrace, NY
March 24, 1965

Lisa M. King-Johnson, 34, New York, NY
November 9, 1966

Takashi Kinoshita, 46, Rye, NY
March 26, 1955

Chris Michael Kirby, 21, New York, NY
January 1, 1980

Howard Barry Kirschbaum, 53, New York, NY
January 24, 1948

Glenn Davis Kirwin, 40, Scarsdale, NY
November 3, 1960

Richard J. Klares, 59, Somers, NY
November 26, 1941

Peter Anton Klein, 35, Weehawken, NJ
May 2, 1966

Alan David Kleinberg, 39, East Brunswick, NJ
November 24, 1961

Karen Joyce Klitzman, 38, New York, NY
November 2, 1962

Ronald Philip Kloepfer, 39, Franklin Square, NY
September 13, 1961

Eugueni Kniazev, 46, New York, NY
December 11, 1954

Andrew James Knox, 30, New York, NY
January 8, 1972

Thomas Patrick Knox, 31, Hoboken, NJ
November 22, 1969

Rebecca Lee Koborie, 48, Guttenberg, NJ
August 10, 1953

Deborah A. Kobus, 36, New York, NY
October 8, 1964

Gary Edward Koecheler, 57, Harrison, NY
February 21, 1944

Frank J. Koestner, 48, New York, NY
August 24, 1953

Ryan Kohart, 26, New York, NY
August 12, 1975

Vanessa Lynn Przybylo Kolpak, 21, New York, NY
October 15, 1979

Irina Kolpakova, 37, New York, NY
January 19, 1964

Suzanne Rose Kondratenko, 27, Chicago, IL
March 3, 1974

Abdoulaye Koné, 37, New York, NY
February 1, 1964

Bon Seok Koo, 42, River Edge, NJ
February 1, 1959

Dorota Kopiczko, 26, Nutley, NJ
June 1, 1975

Scott Michael Kopytko, 32, New York, NY
December 2, 1968

Bojan George Kostic, 34, New York, NY
December 31, 1966

Danielle Kousoulis, 29, New York, NY
September 26, 1971

John J. Kren, 52, New York, NY
December 29, 1948

William Edward Krukowski, 36, New York, NY
January 17, 1965

Lyudmila Ksido, 46, New York, NY
April 11, 1955

Shekhar Kumar, 30, New York, NY
October 14, 1970

Kenneth Bruce Kumpel, 42, Cornwall, NY
December 30, 1958

Frederick Kuo, Jr., 53, Great Neck, NY
April 3, 1948

Patricia Kuras, 42, New York, NY
September 30, 1958

Nauka Kushitani, 44, New York, NY
February 5, 1957

Thomas Joseph Kuveikis, 48, Carmel, NY
March 19, 1953

Victor Kwarkye, 35, New York, NY
September 28, 1965

Raymond Kui Fai Kwok, 31, New York, NY
September 24, 1969

Angela R. Kyte, 49, Boonton Township, NJ
January 18, 1952

L

Amarnauth Lachhman, 42, Valley Stream, NY
December 22, 1959

Andrew La Corte, 61, Jersey City, NJ
February 14, 1940

Ganesh Ladkat, 27, Somerset, NJ
November 13, 1973

James Patrick Ladley, 41, Colts Neck, NJ
September 24, 1959

Joseph A. Lafalce, 54, New York, NY
March 24, 1947

Jeanette Louise LaFond-Menichino, 49, New York, NY
July 19, 1952

David James LaForge, 50, New York, NY
June 11, 1951

Michael Patrick LaForte, 39, Holmdel, NJ
September 11, 1962

Alan Charles Lafrance, 43, New York, NY
July 2, 1958

Juan Mendez Lafuente, 61, Poughkeepsie, NY
June 27, 1940

Neil Kwong-Wah Lai, 59, Hightstown, NJ
January 20, 1942

Vincent Andrew Laieta, 31, Edison, NJ
April 15, 1970

William David Lake, 44, New York, NY
October 30, 1956

Franco Lalama, 45, Nutley, NJ
June 18, 1956

Chow Kwan Lam, 48, Maywood, NJ
February 19, 1953

Stephen LaMantia, 38, Darien, CT
July 14, 1963

Amy Hope Lamonsoff, 29, New York, NY
May 31, 1972

Robert T. Lane, 28, New York, NY
November 28, 1972

Brendan Mark Lang, 30, Red Bank, NJ
October 27, 1970

Rosanne P. Lang, 42, Middletown, NJ
April 27, 1959

Vanessa Langer, 29, Yonkers, NY
October 31, 1971

Mary Lou Langley, 53, New York, NY
December 10, 1947

Peter J. Langone, 41, Roslyn Heights, NY
April 25, 1960

Thomas Michael Langone, 39, Williston Park, NY
July 19, 1962

Michele Bernadette Lanza, 36, New York, NY
April 26, 1965

Ruth Sheila Lapin, 53, East Windsor, NJ
April 16, 1948

Carol Ann La Plante, 59, New York, NY
December 23, 1941

Ingeborg A.D. Lariby, 42, New York, NY
July 5, 1959

Robin Blair Larkey, 48, Chatham, NJ
December 24, 1952

Christopher Randall Larrabee, 26, New York, NY
November 9, 1974

Hamidou S. Larry, 37, New York, NY
February 6, 1964

Scott Larsen, 35, New York, NY
July 25, 1966

John Adam Larson, 37, Colonia, NJ
December 31, 1963

Gary Edward Lasko, 49, Memphis, TN
September 24, 1951

Nicholas Craig Lassman, 28, Cliffside Park, NJ
November 30, 1972

Paul Laszczynski, 49, Paramus, NJ
February 5, 1952

Jeffrey G. La Touche, 49, New York, NY
November 22, 1951

Charles A. Laurencin, 61, New York, NY
July 10, 1940

Stephen James Lauria, 39, New York, NY
December 13, 1961

Maria LaVache, 60, New York, NY
August 28, 1941

Denis Francis Lavelle, 42, Yonkers, NY
January 18, 1959

Jeannine Mary LaVerde, 36, New York, NY
August 2, 1965

Anna A. Laverty, 52, Middletown, NJ
March 1, 1949

Steven Lawn, 28, Princeton, NJ
October 28, 1972

Robert A. Lawrence, Jr., 41, Summit, NJ
April 9, 1960

Nathaniel Lawson, 61, New York, NY
October 2, 1939

Eugen Gabriel Lazar, 27, Glendale, NY
February 28, 1974

James Patrick Leahy, 38, New York, NY
November 26, 1962

Lt. Joseph Gerard Leavey, 45, Pelham, NY
November 13, 1955

Neil J. Leavy, 34, New York, NY
August 19, 1967

Leon Lebor, 51, Jersey City, NJ
July 11, 1950

Kenneth Charles Ledee, 38, Monmouth, NJ
July 17, 1963

Alan J. Lederman, 43, New York, NY
August 19, 1958

Elena F. Ledesma, 36, New York, NY
May 22, 1964

Alexis Leduc, 45, New York, NY
July 16, 1956

David S. Lee, 37, West Orange, NJ
August 11, 1964

Gary H. Lee, 62, Lindenhurst, NY
August 26, 1939

Hyun Joon Lee, 32, New York, NY
December 6, 1968

Juanita Lee, 44, New York, NY
October 6, 1956

Kathryn Blair Lee, 55, New York, NY
April 15, 1946

Linda C. Lee, 34, New York, NY
July 22, 1967

Lorraine M. C. Lee, 37, New York, NY
October 25, 1963

Myoung Woo Lee, 41, Lyndhurst, NJ
December 26, 1959

Richard Y. C. Lee, 34, Great Neck, NY
July 4, 1967

Stuart Soo-Jin Lee, 30, New York, NY
October 31, 1970

Yang Der Lee, 63, New York, NY
November 10, 1937

Stephen Paul Lefkowitz, 50, Belle Harbor, NY
June 9, 1951

Adriana Legro, 32, New York, NY
March 22, 1969

Edward Joseph Lehman, 41, Glen Cove, NY
September 30, 1959

Eric Lehrfeld, 32, New York, NY
July 22, 1969

David Ralph Leistman, 43, Garden City, NY
February 25, 1958

David Prudencio Lemagne, 27, North Bergen, NJ
February 20, 1974

Joseph Anthony Lenihan, 41, Cos Cob, CT
June 9, 1960

John Joseph Lennon, III, 44, Howell, NJ
March 15, 1957

John Robinson Lenoir, 38, Locust Valley, NY
November 20, 1962

Jorge Luis León, Sr., 43, Union City, NJ
September 4, 1958

Matthew G. Leonard, 38, New York, NY
October 24, 1962

Michael Lepore, 39, New York, NY
July 23, 1962

Charles Antoine Lesperance, 55, New York, NY
December 2, 1945

Jeff Earle LeVeen, 55, Manhasset, NY
January 19, 1946

John Dennis Levi, 50, New York, NY
February 23, 1951

Alisha Caren Levin, 33, New York, NY
June 7, 1968

Neil David Levin, 47, New York, NY
September 16, 1954

Robert Levine, 56, West Babylon, NY
March 31, 1945

Robert Michael Levine, 66, Edgewater, NJ
July 20, 1935

Shai Levinhar, 29, New York, NY
May 1, 1972

Adam Jay Lewis, 36, Fairfield, CT
December 19, 1964

Margaret Susan Lewis, 49, Elizabeth, NJ
November 18, 1951

Ye Wei Liang, 27, New York, NY
June 22, 1974

Orasri Liangthanasarn, 26, Bayonne, NJ
May 15, 1975

Daniel F. Libretti, 43, New York, NY
May 6, 1958

Ralph Michael Licciardi, 30, West Hempstead, NY
July 29, 1971

Edward Lichtschein, 35, New York, NY
April 19, 1966

Steven Barry Lillianthal, 38, Millburn, NJ
July 23, 1963

Carlos R. Lillo, 37, North Babylon, NY
November 18, 1963

Craig Damian Lilore, 30, Lyndhurst, NJ
August 25, 1971

Arnold Arboleda Lim, 28, New York, NY
December 24, 1972

Darya Lin, 32, Chicago, IL
August 13, 1969

Wei Rong Lin, 31, Jersey City, NJ
May 1, 1970

Nickie L. Lindo, 31, New York, NY
April 1, 1970

Thomas V. Linehan, Jr., 39, Montville, NJ
December 9, 1961

Robert Thomas Linnane, 33, West Hempstead, NY
April 26, 1968

Alan Patrick Linton, Jr., 26, Port Liberte, NJ
April 22, 1975

Diane Theresa Lipari, 42, New York, NY
August 13, 1959

Kenneth P. Lira Arévalo, 28, Paterson, NJ
December 9, 1972

Francisco Alberto Liriano, 33, New York, NY
January 25, 1968

Lorraine Lisi, 44, New York, NY
June 5, 1957

Paul Lisson, 45, New York, NY
September 2, 1956

Vincent M. Litto, 52, New York, NY
March 13, 1949

Ming-Hao Liu, 41, Livingston, NJ
May 28, 1960

Nancy Liz, 39, New York, NY
September 25, 1962

Harold Lizcano, 31, East Elmhurst, NY
November 29, 1969

Martin Lizzul, 31, New York, NY
January 15, 1970

George A. Llanes, 33, New York, NY
September 13, 1967

Elizabeth Claire Logler, 31, Rockville Centre, NY
October 16, 1969

Catherine Lisa Loguidice, 30, New York, NY
December 5, 1970

Jérôme Robert Lohez, 30, Jersey City, NJ
January 3, 1971

Michael William Lomax, 37, New York, NY
January 16, 1964

Laura Maria Longing, 35, Pearl River, NY
May 3, 1966

Salvatore P. Lopes, 40, Franklin Square, NY
July 30, 1961

Daniel Lopez, 39, New York, NY
July 4, 1962

George Lopez, 40, Stroudsburg, PA
December 25, 1960

Luis Manuel Lopez, 38, New York, NY
July 21, 1962

Manuel L. Lopez, 54, Jersey City, NJ
February 19, 1947

Joseph Lostrangio, 48, Langhorne, PA
June 11, 1958

Chet Dek Louie, 45, New York, NY
December 1, 1957

Stuart Seid Louis, 43, East Brunswick, NJ
July 31, 1958

Joseph Lovero, 60, Jersey City, NJ
September 8, 1941

Michael W. Lowe, 48, New York, NY
May 30, 1953

Garry Lozier, 47, Darien, CT
January 4, 1954

John Peter Lozowsky, 45, Skaneateles Falls, NY
July 4, 1956

Charles Peter Lucania, 34, Long Beach, NY
September 18, 1966

Edward Hobbs Luckett III, 40, Fair Haven, NJ
January 25, 1961

Mark Gavin Ludvigsen, 32, New York, NY
May 12, 1969

Lee Charles Ludwig, 49, New York, NY
November 15, 1951

Sean Thomas Lugano, 28, New York, NY
May 24, 1973

Daniel Lugo, 45, New York, NY
January 11, 1956

Marie Lukas, 32, New York, NY
January 11, 1969

William Lum, Jr., 45, New York, NY
April 25, 1956

Michael P. Lunden, 37, New York, NY
June 15, 1964

Christopher Lunder, 34, Wall, NJ
June 10, 1967

Anthony Luparello, 62, New York, NY
November 24, 1938

Gary Frederick Lutnick, 36, New York, NY
November 3, 1964

Linda Luzzicone, 33, New York, NY
April 26, 1968

Alexander Lygin, 28, New York, NY
January 16, 1973

Farrell Peter Lynch, 39, Centerport, NY
March 7, 1962

James Francis Lynch, 47, Edison, NJ
June 13, 1954

Louise A. Lynch, 58, Amityville, NY
June 3, 1943

Michael Cameron Lynch, 34, New York, NY
October 25, 1966

Michael F. Lynch, 33, New Hyde Park, NY
May 6, 1968

Michael Francis Lynch, 30, New York, NY
December 12, 1970

Richard Dennis Lynch, 30, Bedford Hills, NY
November 18, 1970

Robert Henry Lynch, 44, Cranford, NJ
December 29, 1956

Sean Patrick Lynch, 36, Morristown, NJ
July 26, 1965

Sean P. Lynch, 34, New York, NY
March 4, 1967

Michael J. Lyons, 32, Hawthorne, NY
July 20, 1969

Monica Anne Lyons, 53, New York, NY
July 28, 1948

Patrick John Lyons, 34, Setauket, NY
July 24, 1967

M

Robert Francis Mace, 43, New York, NY
August 19, 1958

Jan Maciejewski, 37, New York, NY
June 24, 1964

Catherine Fairfax MacRae, 23, New York, NY
July 31, 1978

Richard B. Madden, 35, Westfield, NJ
June 30, 1966

Simon Maddison, 40, Florham Park, NJ
March 28, 1961

Noell C. Maerz, 29, Long Beach, NY
September 27, 1971

Jeannieann Maffeo, 40, New York, NY
December 22, 1960

Joseph Maffeo, 30, New York, NY
February 12, 1971

Jay Robert Magazine, 48, New York, NY
June 9, 1953

Brian Magee, 52, Floral Park, NY
June 14, 1949

Charles Wilson Magee, 51, Wantagh, NY
July 21, 1950

Joseph V. Maggitti, 47, Abingdon, MD
March 30, 1954

Ronald E. Magnuson, 57, Park Ridge, NJ
December 21, 1943

Daniel L. Maher, 50, Hamilton, NJ
August 19, 1951

Thomas Anthony Mahon, 37, East Norwich, NY
September 1, 1964

William J. Mahoney, 38, Bohemia, NY
October 16, 1963

Joseph Daniel Maio, 32, Roslyn Harbor, NY
December 21, 1968

Linda C. Mair-Grayling, 44, New York, NY
June 10, 1957

Takashi Makimoto, 49, New York, NY
August 11, 1952

Abdu Ali Malahi, 37, New York, NY
May 3, 1964

Debora I. Maldonado, 47, New York, NY
May 16, 1954

Myrna T. Maldonado-Agosto, 49, New York, NY
April 19, 1952

Alfred Russell Maler, 39, Convent Station, NJ
January 21, 1962

Gregory James Malone, 42, Hoboken, NJ
April 20, 1959

Edward Francis Maloney, 32, Darien, CT
October 11, 1968

Joseph E. Maloney, 46, Farmingville, NY
October 12, 1955

Gene Edward Maloy, 41, New York, NY
January 23, 1960

Christian H. Maltby, 37, Chatham, NJ
February 20, 1964

Francisco Miguel Mancini, 26, New York, NY
September 28, 1974

Joseph Mangano, 53, Jackson, NJ
January 2, 1948

Sara Elizabeth Manley, 31, New York, NY
July 3, 1970

Debra M. Mannetta, 31, Islip, NY
February 5, 1970

Marion Victoria Manning, 27, Rochdale, NY
April 30, 1974

Terence John Manning, 36, Rockville Centre, NY
November 3, 1964

James Maounis, 42, New York, NY
February 5, 1959

Joseph Ross Marchbanks, Jr., 47, Nanuet, NY
June 9, 1954

Peter Edward Mardikian, 29, New York, NY
August 27, 1972

Edward Joseph Mardovich, 42, Lloyd Harbor, NY
February 11, 1959

Lt. Charles Joseph Margiotta, 44, New York, NY
January 15, 1957

Kenneth Joseph Marino, 40, Monroe, NY
July 9, 1961

Lester Vincent Marino, 57, North Massapequa, NY
December 16, 1943

Vita Marino, 49, New York, NY
September 18, 1952

Kevin D. Marlo, 28, New York, NY
January 17, 1973

José J. Marrero, 32, Old Bridge, NJ
November 13, 1968

John Daniel Marshall, 35, Congers, NY
July 23, 1966

James Martello, 41, Rumson, NJ
October 7, 1959

Michael A. Marti, 26, Glendale, NY
February 23, 1975

Lt. Peter C. Martin, 43, Miller Place, NY
August 15, 1958

William J. Martin, Jr., 35, Denville, NJ
August 31, 1966

Brian E. Martineau, 37, Edison, NJ
June 19, 1964

Betsy Martinez, 33, New York, NY
June 19, 1968

Edward J. Martinez, 60, New York, NY
July 11, 1941

José Ángel Martínez, 49, Hauppauge, NY
October 23, 1951

Robert Gabriel Martinez, 24, New York, NY
November 16, 1977

Lizie Martinez-Calderon, 32, New York, NY
September 25, 1968

Lt. Paul Richard Martini, 37, New York, NY
May 8, 1964

Joseph A. Mascali, 44, New York, NY
December 2, 1956

Bernard Mascarenhas, 54, Newmarket, Ontario, Canada
July 15, 1947

Stephen Frank Masi, 55, Selden, NY
September 23, 1945

Nicholas George Massa, 65, New York, NY
February 14, 1936

Patricia Ann Cimaroli Massari, 25, Glendale, NY
August 20, 1976

Michael Massaroli, 38, New York, NY
June 20, 1963

Philip William Mastrandrea, Jr., 42, Chatham, NJ
August 31, 1959

Rudy Mastrocinque, 43, Kings Park, NY
January 8, 1958

Joseph Mathai, 49, Arlington, MA
March 27, 1952

Charles William Mathers, 61, Sea Girt, NJ
July 2, 1940

William A. Mathesen, 40, Morristown, NJ
November 18, 1960

Marcello Matricciano, 31, New York, NY
July 1, 1970

Margaret Elaine Mattic, 51, New York, NY
November 8, 1949

Robert D. Mattson, 54, Green Pond, NJ
November 18, 1946

Walter A. Matuza, Jr., 39, New York, NY
August 4, 1962

Charles A. Mauro, 65, New York, NY
July 9, 1936

Charles J. Mauro, 38, New York, NY
May 16, 1963

Dorothy Mauro, 55, New York, NY
August 30, 1946

Nancy T. Mauro, 51, New York, NY
February 17, 1950

Tyrone May, 44, Rahway, NJ
December 8, 1956

Keithroy Marcellus Maynard, 30, New York, NY
January 22, 1971

Robert J. Mayo, 46, Morganville, NJ
February 14, 1955

Kathy Nancy Mazza, 46, Farmingdale, NY
May 13, 1955

Edward Mazzella, Jr., 62, Monroe, NY
March 26, 1939

Jennifer Lynn Mazzotta, 23, Maspeth, NY
April 12, 1978

Kaaria Mbaya, 39, Edison, NJ
May 12, 1962

James Jospeh McAlary, Jr., 42, Spring Lake Heights, NJ
February 3, 1959

Brian Gerard McAleese, 36, Baldwin, NY
November 24, 1964

Patricia Ann McAneney, 50, Rockland County, NY
April 25, 1951

Colin Richard McArthur, 52, Howell, NJ
June 24, 1949

John Kevin McAvoy, 47, New York, NY
September 17, 1953

Kenneth M. McBrayer, 49, New York, NY
April 15, 1952

Brendan F. McCabe, 40, Sayville, NY
November 12, 1960

Michael McCabe, 42, Rumson, NJ
September 8, 1959

Thomas Joseph McCann, 46, New York, NY
February 19, 1955

Justin McCarthy, 30, Port Washington, NY
September 19, 1971

Kevin M. McCarthy, 42, Fairfield, CT
June 26, 1959

Michael Desmond McCarthy, 33, Huntington, NY
September 8, 1968

Robert Garvin McCarthy, 33, Stony Point, NY
June 29, 1968

Stanley McCaskill, 47, New York, NY
March 28, 1954

Katie Marie McCloskey, 25, Mount Vernon, NY
December 28, 1975

Tara McCloud-Gray, 30, New York, NY
October 23, 1970

Charles Austin McCrann, 55, New York, NY
April 30, 1946

Tonyell F. McDay, 25, Colonia, NJ
June 24, 1976

Matthew T. McDermott, 34, Basking Ridge, NJ
May 27, 1967

Joseph P. McDonald, 43, Livingston, NJ
March 11, 1958

Brian Grady McDonnell, 38, Wantagh, NY
May 21, 1963

Michael P. McDonnell, 34, Middletown, NJ
December 29, 1967

John F. McDowell, Jr., 33, New York, NY
February 16, 1968

Eamon J. McEneaney, 46, New Canaan, CT
December 23, 1954

John Thomas McErlean, Jr., 39, Larchmont, NY
July 27, 1962

Daniel Francis McGinley, 40, Ridgewood, NJ
November 14, 1960

Mark Ryan McGinly, 26, New York, NY
December 24, 1974

Lt. William E. McGinn, 43, New York, NY
June 18, 1958

Thomas Henry McGinnis, 41, Oakland, NJ
June 4, 1960

Michael Gregory McGinty, 42, Foxboro, MA
July 11, 1959

Ann Walsh McGovern, 68, East Meadow, NY
November 25, 1932

Scott Martin McGovern, 35, Wyckoff, NJ
November 29, 1965

William J. McGovern, 49, Smithtown, NY
July 2, 1952

Stacey Sennas McGowan, 38, Basking Ridge, NJ
August 26, 1963

Francis Noel McGuinn, 48, Rye, NY
December 25, 1952

Patrick J. McGuire, 40, Madison, NJ
November 22, 1960

Thomas M. McHale, 33, Huntington, NY
November 27, 1967

Keith David McHeffey, 31, Rumson, NJ
June 12, 1970

Ann M. McHugh, 35, New York, NY
April 15, 1966

Denis J. McHugh III, 36, New York, NY
October 2, 1964

Dennis P. McHugh, 34, Sparkill, NY
February 11, 1967

Michael Edward McHugh, Jr., 35, Tuckahoe, NY
March 9, 1966

Robert G. McIlvaine, 26, New York, NY
November 5, 1974

Donald James McIntyre, 38, New City, NY
December 2, 1962

Stephanie Marie McKenna, 45, New York, NY
July 25, 1956

Barry J. McKeon, 47, Yorktown Heights, NY
September 3, 1954

Evelyn C. McKinnedy, 60, New York, NY
February 9, 1941

Darryl Leron McKinney, 26, New York, NY
December 29, 1974

George Patrick McLaughlin, Jr., 36, Hoboken, NJ
June 23, 1965

Robert C. McLaughlin, 29, Westchester, NY
December 6, 1971

Gavin McMahon, 35, Bayonne, NJ
March 25, 1966

Robert Dismas McMahon, 35, New York, NY
October 23, 1965

Edmund M. McNally, 41, Fair Haven, NJ
October 6, 1960

Daniel Walter McNeal, 29, Jersey City, NJ
March 25, 1972

Walter Arthur McNeil, 53, Stroudsburg, PA
January 10, 1948

Christine Sheila McNulty, 42, Peterborough, England
March 26, 1959

Sean Peter McNulty, 30, New York, NY
July 21, 1971

Robert William McPadden, 30, Pearl River, NY
October 31, 1970

Terence A. McShane, 37, West Islip, NY
August 29, 1964

Timothy Patrick McSweeney, 37, New York, NY
September 5, 1964

Martin E. McWilliams, 35, Kings Park, NY
January 15, 1966

Rocco A. Medaglia, 49, Melville, NY
January 16, 1952

Abigail Cales Medina, 46, New York, NY
April 18, 1955

Ana Iris Medina, 39, New York, NY
October 6, 1961

William J. Meehan, Jr., 49, Darien, CT
December 30, 1951

Damian Meehan, 32, Glen Rock, NJ
May 29, 1969

Alok Kumar Mehta, 23, Hempstead, NY
August 16, 1978

Raymond Meisenheimer, 46, West Babylon, NY
May 6, 1955

Manuel Emilio Mejia, 54, New York, NY
December 23, 1946

Eskedar Melaku, 31, New York, NY
February 28, 1970

Antonio Melendez, 30, New York, NY
June 13, 1971

Mary P. Melendez, 44, Stroudsburg, PA
August 22, 1957

Yelena Melnichenko, 28, New York, NY
July 20, 1973

Stuart Todd Meltzer, 32, Syosset, NY
October 11, 1968

Diarelia Jovannah Mena, 30, New York, NY
August 19, 1971

Charles R. Mendez, 38, Floral Park, NY
March 16, 1963

Lizette Mendoza, 33, North Bergen, NJ
November 22, 1967

Shevonne Olicia Mentis, 25, New York, NY
November 1, 1975

Steve John Mercado, 38, New York, NY
June 1, 1963

Wesley Mercer, 70, New York, NY
August 31, 1931

Ralph Joseph Mercurio, 47, Rockville Centre, NY
October 14, 1953

Alan Harvey Merdinger, 47, Allentown, PA
February 13, 1954

George L. Merino, 39, New York, NY
December 18, 1961

Yamel Josefina Merino, 24, Yonkers, NY
October 21, 1976

George Merkouris, 35, Levittown, NY
November 4, 1965

Deborah Merrick, 45, New York, NY
March 13, 1956

Raymond Joseph Metz, III, 37, Trumbull, CT
July 16, 1964

Jill Ann Metzler, 32, Franklin Square, NY
May 11, 1969

David Robert Meyer, 57, Glen Rock, NJ
December 26, 1943

Nurul Huq Miah, 35, New York, NY
June 2, 1966

William Edward Micciulli, 30, Matawan, NJ
February 6, 1971

Martin Paul Michelstein, 57, Morristown, NJ
April 16, 1944

Luis Clodoaldo Revilla Mier, 54
August 19, 1947

Peter Teague Milano, 43, Middletown, NJ
August 10, 1958

Gregory Milanowycz, 25, Cranford, NJ
August 29, 1976

Lukasz Tomasz Milewski, 21, New York, NY
November 13, 1979

Sharon Christina Millan, 31, New York, NY
December 22, 1969

Craig James Miller, 29, VA
November 4, 1971

Douglas C. Miller, 34, Port Jervis, NY
July 11, 1967

Henry Alfred Miller, Jr., 52, Massapequa, NY
October 18, 1949

Joel Miller, 55, Baldwin, NY
September 17, 1945

Michael Matthew Miller, 39, Englewood, NJ
November 30, 1961

Phillip D. Miller, 53, New York, NY
January 27, 1948

Robert Alan Miller, 46, Old Bridge, NJ
June 2, 1955

Robert Cromwell Miller, Jr., 55, Hasbrouck Heights, NJ
February 21, 1946

Benjamin Millman, 40, New York, NY
August 21, 1961

Charles M. Mills, Jr., 61, Brentwood, NY
November 17, 1939

Ronald Keith Milstein, 54, New York, NY
May 3, 1947

Robert J. Minara, 54, Carmel, NY
July 27, 1947

William George Minardi, 46, Bedford, NY
July 14, 1955

Louis Joseph Minervino, 54, Middletown, NJ
October 10, 1946

Thomas Mingione, 34, West Islip, NY
March 9, 1967

Wilbert Miraille, 29, New York, NY
May 19, 1972

Domenick N. Mircovich, 40, Closter, NJ
February 3, 1961

Rajesh Arjan Mirpuri, 30, Englewood Cliffs, NJ
September 18, 1970

Joseph D. Mistrulli, 47, Wantagh, NY
December 24, 1953

Susan Miszkowicz, 37, New York, NY
November 2, 1963

Lt. Paul Thomas Mitchell, 46, New York, NY
July 17, 1955

Frank V. Moccia, Jr., 57, Hauppauge, NY
January 1, 1944

Richard P. Miuccio, 55, New York, NY
May 23, 1946

Capt. Louis Joseph Modafferi, 45, New York, NY
December 31, 1955

Boyie Mohammed, 50, New York, NY
January 11, 1951

Lt. Dennis Mojica, 50, New York, NY
January 30, 1951

Manuel Mojica, 37, Bellmore, NY
July 6, 1964

Kleber Rolando Molina, 44, New York, NY
November 8, 1956

Manuel De Jesús Molina, 31, New York, NY
December 24, 1969

Carl Molinaro, 32, New York, NY
May 2, 1969

Justin John Molisani, Jr., 42, Lincroft, NJ
October 8, 1958

Brian Patrick Monaghan, 21, New York, NY
August 20, 1980

Franklyn Monahan, 45, Roxbury, NY
November 25, 1955

John Gerard Monahan, 47, Wanamassa, NJ
July 31, 1954

Kristen Leigh Montanaro, 34, New York, NY
August 26, 1967

Craig D. Montano, 38, Glen Ridge, NJ
October 27, 1962

Michael G. Montesi, 39, Highland Mills, NY
January 7, 1962

Cheryl Ann Monyak, 43, Greenwich, CT
December 2, 1957

Capt. Thomas Carlo Moody, 45, Stony Brook, NY
January 3, 1956

Sharon Moore, 37, New York, NY
April 20, 1964

Krishna Moorthy, 59, Briarcliff Manor, NY
May 11, 1942

Abner Morales, 37, New York, NY
September 21, 1963

Carlos Morales, 29, New York, NY
February 8, 1972

Paula E. Morales, 42, New York, NY
March 20, 1959

John Michael Moran, 43, New York, NY
July 16, 1959

John Christopher Moran, 38, Haslemere, Surrey,
    England
May 25, 1963

Kathleen Moran, 42, New York, NY
April 3, 1959

Lindsay Stapleton Morehouse, 24, New York, NY
August 27, 1977

George William Morell, 47, Mount. Kisco, NY
December 2, 1953

Steven P. Morello, 52, Bayonne, NJ
March 17, 1949

Vincent S. Morello, 34, New York, NY
January 6, 1967

Yvette Nicole Moreno, 25, New York, NY
October 4, 1976

Dorothy Morgan, 47, Hempstead, NY
March 12, 1954

Richard J. Morgan, 66, Glen Rock, NJ
June 8, 1935

Nancy Morgenstern, 32, New York, NY
December 10, 1968

Sanae Mori, 27, Tokyo, Japan
April 27, 1974

Blanca Robertina Morocho, 26, New York, NY
September 1, 1975

Leonel Gerónimo Morocho, 36, New York, NY
July 5, 1965

Dennis Gerard Moroney, 39, Eastchester, NY
November 7, 1961

Lynne Irene Morris, 22, Monroe, NY
November 24, 1978

Seth Allan Morris, 35, Kinnelon, NJ
October 17, 1965

Steve Morris, 31, Ormond Beach, FL
May 21, 1970

Christopher M. Morrison, 34, Charlestown, MA
November 16, 1966

Ferdinand V. Morrone, 63, Lake Wood, NJ
May 25, 1938

William David Moskal, 50, Brecksville, OH
August 17, 1951

Marco Motroni, 57, Fort Lee, NJ
May 19, 1945

Cynthia Motus-Wilson, 52, New York, NY
October 18, 1948

Iouri A. Mouchinski, 55, New York, NY
June 11, 1946

Jude Joseph Moussa, 35, New York, NY
October 24, 1965

Peter C. Moutos, 44, Chatham, NJ
February 2, 1957

Damion O'Neil Mowatt, 21, New York, NY
February 22, 1980

Christopher Michael Mozzillo, 27, New York, NY
May 8, 1974

Stephen Vincent Mulderry, 33, New York, NY
May 4, 1968

Richard T. Muldowney, Jr., 40, Babylon, NY
January 13, 1961

Michael D. Mullan, 34, New York, NY
April 6, 1967

Dennis Michael Mulligan, 32, New York, NY
May 6, 1969

Peter James Mulligan, 28, New York, NY
November 5, 1973

Michael Joseph Mullin, 27, Hoboken, NJ
December 3, 1973

James Donald Munhall, 45, Ridgewood, NJ
July 12, 1956

Nancy Muñiz, 45, New York, NY
July 22, 1956

Carlos Mario Muñoz, 43, New York, NY
February 14, 1958

Francisco Muñoz, 29, New York, NY
August 20, 1972

Theresa Munson, 54, New York, NY
February 12, 1947

Robert Michael Murach, 45, Montclair, NJ
July 10, 1956

Cesar Augusto Murillo, 32, New York, NY
January 21, 1969

Marc A. Murolo, 28, New York, NY
February 1, 1973

Mary Catherine Murphy-Boffa, 45, New York, NY
March 29, 1956

Brian Joseph Murphy, 41, New York, NY
March 21, 1960

Charles Anthony Murphy, 38, New York, NY
July 9, 1963

Christopher W. Murphy, 35, Easton, MD
August 8, 1966

Edward Charles Murphy, 42, Clifton, NJ
September 25, 1958

James F. Murphy IV, 30, Garden City, NY
February 12, 1971

James Thomas Murphy, 35, Middletown, NJ
December 8, 1965

Kevin James Murphy, 40, Northport, NY
September 1, 1961

Patrick Sean Murphy, 36, Millburn, NJ
January 29, 1965

Lt. Raymond E. Murphy, 46, New York, NY
December 16, 1954

Robert Eddie Murphy, Jr., 56, New York, NY
June 14, 1945

John Joseph Murray, 32, Hoboken, NJ
September 17, 1968

John Joseph Murray, 52, Colts Neck, NJ
March 7, 1949

Susan D. Murray, 54, Summit, NJ
January 22, 1947

Valerie Victoria Murray, 65, New York, NY
September 15, 1935

Richard Todd Myhre, 37, New York, NY
March 6, 1964

N

Lt. Robert B. Nagel, 55, New York, NY
January 29, 1946

Takuya Nakamura, 30, Tuckahoe, NY
August 13, 1971

Alexander John Robert Napier, 38, Morris Township, NJ
July 7, 1963

Frank Joseph Naples III, 29, Cliffside Park, NJ
October 6, 1971

John Philip Napolitano, 33, Ronkonkoma, NY
July 4, 1968

Catherine Ann Nardella, 40, Bloomfield, NJ
November 21, 1960

Mario Nardone, Jr., 32, New York, NY
July 10, 1969

Manika Narula, 22, Kings Park, NY
October 3, 1978

Narender Nath, 33, Colonia, NJ
March 17, 1969

Karen Susan Navarro, 30, New York, NY
May 27, 1971

Joseph M. Navas, 44, Paramus, NJ
February 12, 1957

Francis Joseph Nazario, 28, Jersey City, NJ
February 10, 1973

Glenroy I. Neblett, 42, New York, NY
September 15, 1958

Rayman Marcus Neblett, 31, Roslyn Heights, NY
August 29, 1970

Jerome O. Nedd, 39, New York, NY
November 4, 1961

Laurence F. Nedell, 51, Lindenhurst, NY
November 13, 1948

Luke G. Nee, 44, Stony Point, NY
June 25, 1957

Pete Negron, 34, Bergenfield, NJ
September 19, 1966

Ann Nicole Nelson, 30, New York, NY
May 17, 1971

David William Nelson, 50, New York, NY
April 8, 1951

James A. Nelson, 40, Clark, NJ
July 10, 1961

Michele Ann Nelson, 27, North Valley Stream, NY
December 7, 1973

Peter Allen Nelson, 42, Huntington Station, NY
October 7, 1958

Oscar Francis Nesbitt, 58, New York, NY
April 1, 1943

Gerard Terence Nevins, 46, Campbell Hall, NY
February 21, 1955

Christopher Newton-Carter, 51, Middletown, NJ
December 17, 1949

Nancy Yuen Ngo, 36, Harrington Park, NJ
January 26, 1965

Jody Tepedino Nichilo, 39, New York, NY
September 9, 1962

Martin Stewart Niederer, 23, Hoboken, NJ
September 26, 1977

Alfonse Joseph Niedermeyer, 40, Manasquan, NJ
April 17, 1961

Frank John Niestadt, Jr., 55, Ronkonkoma, NY
August 7, 1946

Gloria Nieves, Jr., 48, New York, NY
September 21, 1952

Juan Nieves, 56, New York, NY
February 7, 1945

Troy Edward Nilsen, 33, New York, NY
March 2, 1968

Paul Nimbley, 42, Middletown, NJ
August 15, 1959

John Ballantine Niven, 44, New York, NY
July 5, 1957

Katherine McGarry Noack, 30, Hoboken, NJ
November 14, 1971

Curtis Terrence Noel, 22, New York, NY
January 2, 1979

Daniel R. Nolan, 44, Hopatcong, NJ
December 29, 1956

Robert Walter Noonan, 36, Greenwich, CT
April 27, 1965

Daniela Rosalia Notaro, 25, New York, NY
April 23, 1976

Brian Christopher Novotny, 33, Hoboken, NJ
December 28, 1967

Soichi Numata, 45, Irvington, NY
October 9, 1955

Brian Nuñez, 29, New York, NY
March 31, 1972

José R. Nuñez, 42, New York, NY
October 5, 1958

Jeffrey Roger Nussbaum, 37, Oceanside, NY
December 20, 1963

O

James A. Oakley, 52, Cortlandt Manor, NY
July 22, 1949

Dennis Patrick O'Berg, 28, Babylon, NY
July 31, 1973

James P. O'Brien, Jr., 33, New York, NY
July 24, 1968

Michael P. O'Brien, 42, Cedar Knolls, NJ
May 14, 1959

Scott J. O'Brien, 40, New York, NY
February 14, 1961

Timothy Michael O'Brien, 40, Brookville, NY
July 5, 1961

Captain Daniel O'Callaghan, 42, Smithtown, NY
February 3, 1959

Diana J. O'Connor, 38, Eastchester, NY
October 8, 1963

Keith Kevin O'Connor, 28, Hoboken, NJ
October 28, 1972

Richard J. O'Connor, 49, LaGrangeville, NY
March 26, 1952

Amy O'Doherty, 23, New York, NY
December 21, 1977

Marni Pont O'Doherty, 31, Armonk, NY
March 27, 1970

Douglas Oelschlager, 36, New York, NY
March 5, 1965

Takashi Ogawa, 37, Tokyo, Japan
May 14, 1964

Albert Ogletree, 49, New York, NY
December 25, 1951

Philip Paul Ognibene, 39, New York, NY
March 16, 1962

James Andrew O'Grady, 32, Harrington Park, NJ
May 9, 1969

Joseph J. Ogren, 30, New York, NY
December 28, 1970

Lt. Thomas O'Hagan, 43, New York, NY
May 28, 1958

Samuel Oitice, 45, Peekskill, NY
April 24, 1956

Patrick J. O'Keefe, 44, Oakdale, NY
July 17, 1957

Capt. William O'Keefe, 49, New York, NY
October 15, 1952

Gerald Michael Olcott, 55, New Hyde Park, NY
March 12, 1946

Gerald Thomas O'Leary, 34, Stony Point, NY
May 26, 1967

Christine Anne Olender, 39, New York, NY
July 4, 1962

Elsy Carolina Osorio Oliva, 27, New York, NY
August 19, 1974

Linda Mary Oliva, 44, New York, NY
November 15, 1956

Edward K. Oliver, 31, Jackson, NJ
January 11, 1970

Leah E. Oliver, 24, New York, NY
September 12, 1976

Eric Taube Olsen, 41, New York, NY
November 17, 1959

Jeffrey James Olsen, 31, New York, NY
June 26, 1970

Maureen Lyons Olson, 50, Rockville Centre, NY
October 12, 1950

Steven John Olson, 38, New York, NY
August 19, 1963

Matthew Timothy O'Mahony, 39, New York, NY
April 29, 1962

Toshihiro Onda, 39, New York, NY
October 21, 1961

Seamus L. Oneal, 52, New York, NY
May 5, 1949

John P. O'Neill, 49, New York, NY
February 6, 1952

Peter J. O'Neill, 21, Valley Stream, NY
November 27, 1979

Sean Gordon Corbett O'Neill, 34, Rye, NY
May 24, 1967

Michael C. Opperman, 45, Selden, NY
February 27, 1956

Christopher T. Orgielewicz, 35, Larchmont, NY
October 15, 1965

Margaret Quinn Orloske, 50, Windsor, CT
August 16, 1951

Virginia Anne Ormiston, 42, New York, NY
April 3, 1959

Kevin M. O'Rourke, 44, Hewlett, NY
July 26, 1957

Ronald Orsini, 59, Hillsdale, NJ
August 17, 1942

Peter Keith Ortale, 37, New York, NY
May 19, 1964

Alexander Ortiz, 36, Ridgewood, NY
April 24, 1965

David Ortiz, 37, Nanuet, NY
April 8, 1964

Emilio Pete Ortiz, 38, New York, NY
November 5, 1962

Pablo Ortiz, 49, New York, NY
January 25, 1952

Paul Ortiz, Jr., 21, New York, NY
January 31, 1980

Sonia Ortiz, 58, New York, NY
June 26, 1943

Masaru Ose, 36, Fort Lee, NJ
August 25, 1965

Patrick J. O'Shea, 45, Farmingdale, NY
January 27, 1956

Robert W. O'Shea, 47, Wall, NJ
January 25, 1954

James Robert Ostrowski, 37, Garden City, NY
May 8, 1964

Timothy Franklin O'Sullivan, 68, Albrightsville, PA
March 5, 1933

Jason Douglas Oswald, 28, New York, NY
December 18, 1972

Michael John Otten, 42, East Islip, NY
February 21, 1959

Isidro D. Ottenwalder, 35, New York, NY
May 15, 1966

Michael Chung Ou, 53, New York, NY
September 19, 1947

Todd Joseph Ouida, 25, River Edge, NJ
May 18, 1976

Jesús Ovalles, 60, New York, NY
June 20, 1941

Peter J. Owens, Jr., 42, Williston Park, NY
December 2, 1958

Adianes Oyola, 23, New York, NY
August 9, 1978

Angel M. Pabon, Jr., 54, New York, NY
May 26, 1948

P

Israel Pabon, Jr., 31, New York, NY
January 18, 1970

Roland Pacheco, 25, New York, NY
October 12, 1975

Michael Benjamin Packer, 45, Hartsdale, NY
February 20, 1956

Deepa K. Pakkala, 31, Stewartsville, NJ
August 17, 1970

Jeffrey Matthew Palazzo, 33, New York, NY
November 25, 1967

Thomas Anthony Palazzo, 44, Armonk, NY
August 21, 1957

Richard A. Palazzolo, 39, New York, NY
February 18, 1962

Orio Joseph Palmer, 45, Valley Stream, NY
March 2, 1956

Frank Anthony Palombo, 46, New York, NY
March 14, 1955

Alan N. Palumbo, 42, New York, NY
September 13, 1959

Christopher Matthew Panatier, 36, Rockville Centre, NY
May 5, 1965

Dominique Lisa Pandolfo, 27, Hoboken, NJ
March 18, 1974

Paul J. Pansini, 34, New York, NY
October 10, 1965

John M. Paolillo, 51, Glen Head, NY
February 28, 1950

Edward Joseph Papa, 47, Oyster Bay, NY
July 1, 1954

Salvatore Papasso, 34, New York, NY
April 1, 1967

James Nicholas Pappageorge, 29, Yonkers, NY
March 23, 1972

Vinod K. Parakat, 34, Sayreville, NJ
April 26, 1967

Vijayashanker Paramsothy, 23, New York, NY
October 30, 1977

Nitin Ramesh Parandkar, 28, Woodbridge, NJ
November 27, 1973

Hardai (Casey) Parbhu, 42, New York, NY
November 20, 1958

James Wendell Parham, 32, New York, NY
September 13, 1968

Debra Marie Paris, 48, New York, NY
February 16, 1953

George Paris, 33, Carmel, NY
November 11, 1967

Gye Hyong Park, 28, New York, NY
October 8, 1972

Philip L. Parker, 53, Skillman, NJ
November 25, 1947

Michael Alaine Parkes, 27, New York, NY
February 4, 1974

Robert E. Parks, Jr., 47, Middletown, NJ
April 22, 1954

Hasmukhrai Chuckulal Parmar, 48, Warren, NJ
January 3, 1953

Robert Parro, 35, Levittown, NY
February 11, 1966

Diane Marie Moore Parsons, 58, Malta, NY
July 14, 1943

Leobardo Lopez Pascual, 41, New York, NY
June 16, 1959

Michael J. Pascuma, 50, Massapequa Park, NY
January 8, 1951

Jerrold Hughes Paskins, 56, Anaheim Hills, CA
April 2, 1944

Horace Robert Passananti, 55, New York, NY
September 24, 1945

Suzanne H. Passaro, 38, East Brunswick, NJ
May 12, 1963

Dipti Patel, 38, New Hyde Park, NY
September 5, 1963

Manish K. Patel, 29, Edison, NJ
October 15, 1971

Steven Bennett Paterson, 40, Ridgewood, NJ
January 21, 1961

James Matthew Patrick, 30, Norwalk, CT
October 13, 1970

Manuel D. Patrocino, 34, New York, NY
February 8, 1967

Bernard E. Patterson, 46, Upper Brookville, NY
July 14, 1955

Cira Marie Patti, 40, New York, NY
April 21, 1961

Robert Edward Pattison, 40, New York, NY
October 30, 1960

James Robert Paul, 58, New York, NY
July 21, 1943

Patrice Paz, 52, New York, NY
September 21, 1949

Victor Hugo Paz, 43, New York, NY
April 1, 1958

Stacey Lynn Peak, 36, New York, NY
September 4, 1965

Richard Allen Pearlman, 18, New York, NY
March 7, 1983

Durrell V. Pearsall, Jr., 34, Hempstead, NY
August 19, 1967

Thomas E. Pedicini, 30, Woodside, NY
May 18, 1971

Todd Douglas Pelino, 34, Fair Haven, NJ
February 15, 1967

Michel Adrian Pelletier, 36, Greenwich, CT
January 30, 1965

Anthony G. Peluso, 46, New York, NY
November 26, 1954

Angel Ramón Pena, 45, River Vale, NJ
October 13, 1955

Richard Al Penny, 53, New York, NY
June 3, 1948

Salvatore F. Pepe, 45, New York, NY
January 29, 1956

Carl Allen Peralta, 37, New York, NY
August 9, 1964

Robert David Peraza, 30, New York, NY
May 26, 1971

Jon A. Perconti, Jr., 32, Brick, NJ
May 17, 1969

Alejo Perez, 66, Union City, NJ
June 10, 1935

Angel Perez, Jr., 43, Jersey City, NJ
November 3, 1959

Angela Susan Perez, 35, New York, NY
July 30, 1966

Anthony Perez, 33, Locust Valley, NY
March 31, 1968

Ivan Antonio Perez, 37, New York, NY
December 8, 1963

Nancy E. Perez, 36, Secaucus, NJ
February 12, 1965

Joseph John Perroncino, 33, Smithtown, NY
March 6, 1968

Edward J. Perrotta, 43, Mount Sinai, NY
September 1, 1958

Emelda H. Perry, 52, Elmont, NY
June 14, 1949

Lt. Glenn C. Perry, Sr., 41, Monroe, NY
July 10, 1960

John William Perry, 38, New York, NY
June 24, 1963

Franklin Allan Pershep, 59, New York, NY
March 30, 1942

Danny Pesce, 34, New York, NY
July 26, 1967

Michael John Pescherine, 32, New York, NY
December 27, 1968

Davin Peterson, 25, New York, NY
June 3, 1976

William Russel Peterson, 46, New York, NY
January 6, 1955

Mark James Petrocelli, 28, New York, NY
September 13, 1972

Lt. Philip S. Petti, 43, New York, NY
August 10, 1958

Glen Kerrin Pettit, 30, Ronkonkoma, NY
June 9, 1971

Dominick A. Pezzulo, 36, New York, NY
August 15, 1965

Kaleen Elizabeth Pezzuti, 28, Fair Haven, NJ
January 31, 1973

Lt. Kevin Pfeifer, 42, New York, NY
July 10, 1959

Tu-Anh Pham, 42, Princeton, NJ
July 1, 1959

Lt. Kenneth John Phelan, Sr., 41, Maspeth, NY
June 27, 1960

Eugenia McCann Piantieri, 55, New York, NY
September 6, 1946

Ludwig John Picarro, 44, Basking Ridge, NJ
April 1, 1957

Matthew Picerno, 44, Holmdel, NJ
May 4, 1957

Joseph O. Pick, 40, Hoboken, NJ
August 16, 1961

Christopher J. Pickford, 32, Glendale, NY
June 15, 1969

Dennis J. Pierce, 54, New York, NY
November 16, 1946

Nicholas P. Pietrunti, 38, Middletown, NJ
July 2, 1963

Theodoros Pigis, 60, New York, NY
November 18, 1940

Susan Elizabeth Ancona Pinto, 44, New York, NY
November 20, 1956

Joseph Piskadlo, 48, North Arlington, NJ
April 13, 1953

Christopher Todd Pitman, 30, New York, NY
August 24, 1971

Josh Michael Piver, 23, New York, NY
June 25, 1978

Joseph Plumitallo, 45, Manalapan, NJ
May 17, 1956

John M. Pocher, 36, Middletown, NJ
November 9, 1964

William Howard Pohlmann, 56, Ardsley, NY
December 16, 1944

Laurence Michael Polatsch, 32, New York, NY
October 9, 1968

Thomas H. Polhemus, 39, Morris Plains, NJ
November 17, 1961

Steve Pollicino, 48, Plainview, NY
February 2, 1953

Susan M. Pollio, 45, Long Beach Township, NJ
January 18, 1956

Joshua Iosua Poptean, 37, New York, NY
April 14, 1964

Giovanna Porras, 24, New York, NY
September 1, 1977

Anthony Portillo, 48, New York, NY
May 11, 1953

James Edward Potorti, 52, Princeton, NJ
July 21, 1949

Daphne Pouletsos, 47, Westwood, NJ
March 4, 1954

Richard Poulos, 55, Levittown, NY
January 5, 1946

Stephen E. Poulos, 45, Basking Ridge, NJ
October 23, 1955

Brandon Jerome Powell, 26, New York, NY
July 30, 1975

Shawn Edward Powell, 32, New York, NY
June 28, 1969

Antonio Dorsey Pratt, 43, New York, NY
January 5, 1958

Gregory M. Preziose, 34, Holmdel, NJ
March 24, 1967

Wanda Ivelisse Prince, 30, New York, NY
November 17, 1970

Vincent A. Princiotta, 39, Orangeburg, NY
November 20, 1961

Kevin M. Prior, 28, Bellmore, NY
January 18, 1973

Everett Martin Proctor III, 44, New York, NY
September 2, 1957

Carrie Beth Progen, 25, Ashburham, MA
March 23, 1976

David Lee Pruim, 53, Upper Montclair, NJ
March 24, 1948

Richard Prunty, 57, Sayville, NY
January 18, 1944

John Foster Puckett, 47, Glen Cove, NY
February 21, 1954

Robert David Pugliese, 47, East Fishkill, NY
June 10, 1954

Edward F. Pullis, 34, Hazlet, NJ
July 22, 1967

Patricia Ann Puma, 33, New York, NY
May 4, 1968

Hemanth Kumar Puttur, 26, White Plains, NY
December 13, 1973

Edward R. Pykon, 33, West Windsor, NJ
May 28, 1968

Q
Christopher Quackenbush, 44, Manhasset, NY
January 5, 1957

Lars Peter Qualben, 49, New York, NY
December 7, 1951

Lincoln Quappé, 38, Sayville, NY
May 2, 1963

Beth Ann Quigley, 25, New York, NY
September 25, 1975

Lt. Michael Quilty, 42, New York, NY
October 11, 1958

James Francis Quinn, 23, New York, NY
November 6, 1977

Ricardo Quinn, 40, New York, NY
April 10, 1961

R
Carol Millicent Rabalais, 38, New York, NY
May 7, 1963

Christopher Peter Anthony Racaniello, 30, Douglaston, NY
August 20, 1971

Leonard J. Ragaglia, 36, New York, NY
June 8, 1965

Eugene J. Raggio, 55, New York, NY
April 7, 1946

Laura Marie Ragonese-Snik, 41, Bangor, PA
August 29, 1960

Michael Paul Ragusa, 29, New York, NY
July 30, 1972

Peter Frank Raimondi, 46, New York, NY
April 23, 1955

Harry A. Raines, 37, Bethpage, NY
September 15, 1963

Ehtesham U. Raja, 28, Clifton, NJ
January 18, 1973

Valsa Raju, 39, Yonkers, NY
May 28, 1961

Edward J. Rall, 44, Holbrook, NY
April 11, 1957

Lukas Rambousek, 27, New York, NY
January 6, 1974

Maria Ramirez, 25, New York, NY
September 30, 1975

Harry Ramos, 41, Newark, NJ
September 16, 1955

Vishnoo Ramsaroop, 44, New York, NY
November 27, 1956

Lorenzo E. Ramzey, 48, Northport, NY
March 20, 1953

Alfred Todd Rancke, 42, Summit, NJ
December 23, 1958

Adam David Rand, 30, Bellmore, NY
July 23, 1971

Jonathan C. Randall, 42, New York, NY
February 1, 1959

Shreyas S. Ranganath, 26, Hackensack, NJ
January 4, 1975

Anne Rose T. Ransom, 45, Edgewater, NJ
March 8, 1956

Faina Rapoport, 45, New York, NY
November 16, 1955

Robert Arthur Rasmussen, 42, Hinsdale, IL
November 14, 1958

Amenia Rasool, 33, New York, NY
March 4, 1968

R. Mark Rasweiler, 53, Flemington, NJ
February 3, 1948

David Alan James Rathkey, 47, Mountain Lakes, NJ
April 28, 1954

William Ralph Raub, 38, Saddle River, NJ
January 9, 1963

Gerard F. Rauzi, 42, New York, NY
March 24, 1959

Alexey Razuvaev, 40, New York, NY
August 17, 1961

Gregory Reda, 33, New Hyde Park, NY
December 19, 1967

Sarah Anne Redheffer, 35, London, England
July 26, 1966

Michele Marie Reed, 26, Ringoes, NJ
July 9, 1975

Judith Ann Reese, 56, Kearny, NJ
November 3, 1944

Donald J. Regan, 47, Pine Bush, NY
November 16, 1953

Lt. Robert M. Regan, 48, Floral Park, NY
May 31, 1953

Thomas M. Regan, 43, Cranford, NJ
January 26, 1958

Christian Michael Otto Regenhard, 28, New York, NY
August 25, 1973

Howard Reich, 59, New York, NY
June 20, 1942

Gregg Reidy, 26, Holmdel, NJ
October 12, 1975

Kevin O. Reilly, 28, New York, NY
August 4, 1973

James Brian Reilly, 25, New York, NY
April 2, 1976

Timothy E. Reilly, 40, New York, NY
October 5, 1960

Joseph Reina, Jr., 32, New York, NY
May 31, 1969

Thomas Barnes Reinig, 48, Bernardsville, NJ
June 8, 1953

Frank Bennett Reisman, 41, Princeton, NJ
November 29, 1959

Joshua Scott Reiss, 23, New York, NY
March 9, 1978

Karen Renda, 52, New York, NY
February 8, 1949

John Armand Reo, 28, Larchmont, NY
January 25, 1973

Richard Cyril Rescorla, 62, Morristown, NJ
May 27, 1939

John Thomas Resta, 40, New York, NY
July 23, 1961

Sylvia San Pio Resta, 26, New York, NY
September 27, 1974

Eduvigis (Eddie) Reyes, 37, New York, NY
March 24, 1964

Bruce Albert Reynolds, 41, Columbia, NJ
July 31, 1960

John Frederick Rhodes, 57, Howell, NJ
June 13, 1944

Francis Saverio Riccardelli, 40, Westwood, NJ
December 28, 1960

Rudolph N. Riccio, 50, New York, NY
April 28, 1950

Ann Marie Riccoboni, 58, New York, NY
September 11, 1943

David Harlow Rice, 31, New York, NY
December 22, 1969

Eileen Mary Rice, 57, New York, NY
July 31, 1944

Kenneth Frederick Rice, III, 34, Hicksville, NY
June 5, 1967

Lt. Vernon Allan Richard, 53, Nanuet, NY
October 20, 1947

Claude Daniel Richards, 46, New York, NY
March 4, 1955

Gregory Richards, 30, New York, NY
December 28, 1970

Michael Richards, 38, New York, NY
August 2, 1963

Venesha Orintia Richards, 26, North Brunswick, NJ
November 30, 1974

Jimmy Riches, 29, New York, NY
September 12, 1971

Alan Jay Richman, 44, New York, NY
July 23, 1957

John M. Rigo, 48, New York, NY
May 15, 1953

Ginger Risco Nelson, 48, New York, NY
June 9, 1953

Rose Mary Riso, 55, New York, NY
February 14, 1946

Moises N. Rivas, 29, New York, NY
January 12, 1972

Joseph R. Rivelli, Jr., 43, New York, NY
January 5, 1958

Carmen Alicia Rivera, 33, Westtown, NY
August 22, 1968

Isaias Rivera, 51, Perth Amboy, NJ
March 8, 1950

Juan William Rivera, 27, New York, NY
October 8, 1973

Linda Ivelisse Rivera, 26, New York, NY
August 22, 1975

David E. Rivers, 40, New York, NY
March 1, 1961

Joseph R. Riverso, 34, White Plains, NY
May 6, 1967

Paul V. Rizza, 34, Park Ridge, NJ
June 1, 1967

John Frank Rizzo, 50, New York, NY
July 28, 1951

Stephen Louis Roach, 36, Verona, NJ
October 15, 1964

Joseph Roberto, 37, Midland Park, NJ
March 31, 1964

Leo Arthur Roberts, 44, Wayne, NJ
August 10, 1957

Michael E. Roberts, 30, New York, NY
July 15, 1970

Michael Edward Roberts, 30, Pearl River, NY
December 22, 1970

Donald Walter Robertson, Jr., 35, Rumson, NJ
December 24, 1965

Catherina Henry-Robinson, 45, New York, NY
October 22, 1955

Jeffrey Robinson, 38, Monmouth Junction, NJ
October 27, 1962

Michell Lee Jean Robotham, 32, Kearny, NJ
January 18, 1969

Donald Arthur Robson, 52, Plandome, NY
May 30, 1949

Antonio A. Rocha, 34, East Hanover, NJ
February 8, 1967

Raymond James Rocha, 29, Hoboken, NJ
March 27, 1972

Laura Rockefeller, 41, New York, NY
October 13, 1959

John Michael Rodak, 39, Sewell, NJ
September 29, 1961

Antonio José Rodrigues, 35, Port Washington, NY
June 2, 1966

Anthony Rodriguez, 36, New York, NY
December 14, 1964

Carmen Milagros Rodriguez, 46, Freehold, NJ
January 15, 1955

Gregory E. Rodriguez, 31, New York, NY
November 12, 1969

Marsha A. Rodriguez, 41, West Paterson, NJ
June 9, 1960

Richard Rodriguez, 31, Cliffwood, NJ
July 2, 1970

David Bartolo Rodriguez-Vargas, 44, New York, NY
May 17, 1957

Matthew Rogan, 37, West Islip, NY
June 20, 1964

Karlie Rogers, 25, London, England
May 30, 1975

Scott William Rohner, 22, River Edge, NJ
March 23, 1979

Keith Michael Roma, 27, New York, NY
April 16, 1974

Joseph M. Romagnolo, 37, Coram, NY
June 27, 1964

Efrain Romero, Sr., 57, Hazleton, PA
April 10, 1944

Elvin Romero, 34, Matawan, NJ
January 26, 1967

James A. Romito, 51, Washington Township, NJ
July 26, 1950

Sean Paul Rooney, 50, Stamford, CT
February 15, 1951

Eric Thomas Ropiteau, 24, New York, NY
April 19, 1977

Aida Rosario, 42, Jersey City, NJ
December 13, 1958

Angela Rosario, 27, New York, NY
November 2, 1973

Mark H. Rosen, 45, West Islip, NY
March 2, 1956

Brooke David Rosenbaum, 31, Franklin Square, NY
December 27, 1969

Linda Rosenbaum, 41, Little Falls, NJ
April 21, 1960

Sheryl Lynn Rosenbaum, 33, Warren, NJ
March 2, 1968

Lloyd Daniel Rosenberg, 31, Morganville, NJ
December 11, 1969

Mark Louis Rosenberg, 26, Teaneck, NJ
December 9, 1974

Andrew Ira Rosenblum, 45, Rockville Centre, NY
August 20, 1956

Joshua M. Rosenblum, 28, Hoboken, NJ
April 30, 1973

Joshua Alan Rosenthal, 44, New York, NY
June 4, 1957

Richard David Rosenthal, 50, Fair Lawn, NJ
May 17, 1951

Daniel Rosetti, 32, Bloomfield, NJ
January 5, 1969

Norman S. Rossinow, 39, Cedar Grove, NJ
January 23, 1962

Nicholas P. Rossomando, 35, New York, NY
May 26, 1966

Michael Craig Rothberg, 39, Old Greenwich, CT
May 27, 1962

Donna Marie Rothenberg, 53, New York, NY
June 2, 1948

Nicholas Charles Alexander Rowe, 29, Hoboken, NJ
March 17, 1973

Timothy Alan Roy, Sr., 36, Massapequa Park, NY
May 9, 1965

Paul G. Ruback, 50, Newburgh, NY
July 24, 1951

Ronald J. Ruben, 36, Hoboken, NJ
February 4, 1965

Joanne Rubino, 45, New York, NY
September 5, 1956

David Michael Ruddle, 31, New York, NY
January 30, 1970

Bart Joseph Ruggiere, 32, New York, NY
October 15, 1968

Susan Ann Ruggiero, 30, Plainview, NY
October 21, 1970

Adam Keith Ruhalter, 40, Plainview, NY
June 9, 1960

Gilbert Ruiz, 57, New York, NY
August 12, 1944

Stephen P. Russell, 40, New York, NY
May 19, 1961

Steven Harris Russin, 32, Mendham, NJ
June 7, 1969

Lt. Michael Thomas Russo, Sr., 44, Nesconset, NY
June 22, 1957

Wayne Alan Russo, 37, Union, NJ
January 5, 1964

Edward Ryan, 42, Scarsdale, NY
September 29, 1958

John Joseph Ryan, 45, Princeton Junction, NJ
June 9, 1956

Jonathan Stephan Ryan, 32, Bayville, NY
December 21, 1968

Kristin A. Irvine Ryan, 30, New York, NY
May 22, 1971

Matthew L. Ryan, 54, Seaford, NY
June 23, 1947

Tatiana Ryjova, 36, South Salem, NY
February 23, 1965

Christina Sunga Ryook, 25, New York, NY
November 15, 1975

S

Thierry Saada, 27, New York, NY
January 11, 1975

Jason Elazar Sabbag, 26, New York, NY
April 30, 1975

Thomas E. Sabella, 44, New York, NY
June 20, 1957

Scott H. Saber, 36, New York, NY
September 20, 1964

Joseph Francis Sacerdote, 48, Freehold, NJ
March 18, 1953

Francis John Sadocha, 41, Huntington, NY
May 3, 1960

Jude Elias Safi, 24, New York, NY
October 9, 1976

Brock Joel Safronoff, 26, New York, NY
May 16, 1975

Edward Saiya, 49, New York, NY
November 1, 1951

John Patrick Salamone, 37, North Caldwell, NJ
January 25, 1964

Hernando Rafael Salas, 71, New York, NY
April 15, 1930

Juan G. Salas, 35, New York, NY
September 25, 1965

Esmerlin Antonio Salcedo, 36, New York, NY
September 5, 1965

John Pepe Salerno, 31, Westfield, NJ
September 6, 1970

Richard L. Salinardi, Jr., 32, Hoboken, NJ
May 17, 1969

Wayne John Saloman, 43, Seaford, NY
April 25, 1958

Nolbert Salomon, 33, New York, NY
September 13, 1967

Catherine Patricia Salter, 37, New York, NY
August 24, 1964

Frank Salvaterra, 41, Manhasset, NY
October 4, 1959

Paul Richard Salvio, 27, New York, NY
February 1, 1974

Samuel Robert Salvo, Jr., 59, Yonkers, NY
May 13, 1942

Carlos Alberto Samaniego, 29, New York, NY
December 31, 1971

Rena Sam Dinnoo, 28, New York, NY
January 7, 1973

James Kenneth Samuel, Jr., 29, Hoboken, NJ
September 27, 1971

Michael V. San Phillip, 55, Ridgewood, NJ
November 16, 1945

Hugo M. Sanay, 41, New York, NY
January 21, 1960

Alva Cynthia Jeffries Sanchez, 41, Hempstead, NY
April 18, 1960

Jacquelyn P. Sanchez, 23, New York, NY
October 23, 1977

Eric M. Sand, 36, Westchester, NY
May 19, 1965

Stacey Leigh Sanders, 25, New York, NY
March 22, 1976

Herman S. Sandler, 57, New York, NY
March 2, 1944

Jim Sands, Jr., 39, Brick, NJ
May 24, 1963

Ayleen J. Santiago, 40, New York, NY
July 31, 1961

Kirsten Reese Santiago, 26, New York, NY
March 29, 1975

Maria Theresa Concepcion Santillan, 27, Morris Plains, NJ
May 16, 1974

Susan Gayle Santo, 24, New York, NY
September 22, 1976

Christopher A. Santora, 23, New York, NY
September 19, 1977

John August Santore, 49, New York, NY
February 3, 1952

Mario L. Santoro, 28, New York, NY
March 17, 1973

Rafael Humberto Santos, 42, New York, NY
June 15, 1959

Rufino C. F. Santos III, 37, New York, NY
February 19, 1964

Kalyan K. Sarkar, 53, Westwood, NJ
September 29, 1947

Chapelle Renee Stewart Sarker, 37, New York, NY
September 28, 1963

Paul F. Sarle, 38, Babylon, NY
January 5, 1963

Deepika Kumar Sattaluri, 33, Edison, NJ
May 6, 1968

Gregory Thomas Saucedo, 31, New York, NY
December 16, 1969

Susan M. Sauer, 48, Chicago, IL
November 21, 1952

Anthony Savas, 72, New York, NY
October 8, 1928

Vladimir Savinkin, 21, New York, NY
May 9, 1980

John Michael Sbarbaro, 45, New York, NY
April 3, 1956

Robert Louis Scandole, 36, Pelham, NY
February 9, 1965

Michelle Scarpitta, 26, New York, NY
July 16, 1975

Dennis Scauso, 46, Dix Hills, NY
June 11, 1955

John Albert Schardt, 34, New York, NY
January 2, 1967

John G. Scharf, 29, Manorville, NY
June 2, 1972

Fred C. Scheffold, Jr., 57, Piermont, NY
December 11, 1943

Angela Susan Scheinberg, 46, New York, NY
January 6, 1955

Scott Mitchell Schertzer, 28, Edison, NJ
December 17, 1972

Sean Schielke, 27, New York, NY
December 18, 1973

Steven Francis Schlag, 41, Franklin Lakes, NJ
April 17, 1960

Jon Schlissel, 51, Jersey City, NJ
March 10, 1950

Karen Helene Schmidt, 42, Bellmore, NY
December 30, 1958

Ian Schneider, 45, Short Hills, NJ
January 8, 1956

Thomas G. Schoales, 27, Stony Point, NY
August 2, 1974

Marisa Dinardo Schorpp, 38, White Plains, NY
December 31, 1962

Frank G. Schott, Jr., 39, Massapequa Park, NY
November 17, 1961

Gerard Patrick Schrang, 45, Holbrook, NY
January 24, 1956

Jeffrey H. Schreier, 48, New York, NY
January 30, 1953

John T. Schroeder, 31, Hoboken, NJ
June 7, 1970

Susan Lee Schuler, 55, Allentown, NJ
May 9, 1946

Edward W. Schunk, 54, Baldwin, NY
April 6, 1947

Mark Evan Schurmeier, 44, McLean, VA
August 20, 1957

John Burkhardt Schwartz, 49, New York, NY
April 16, 1952

Mark Schwartz, 50, West Hempstead, NY
March 15, 1951

Adriane Victoria Scibetta, 31, New York, NY
April 21, 1970

Raphael Scorca, 61, Beachwood, NJ
July 31, 1940

Randolph Scott, 48, Stamford, CT
May 27, 1953

Christopher Jay Scudder, 34, Monsey, NY
October 9, 1966

Arthur Warren Scullin, 57, New York, NY
May 7, 1944

Michael H. Seaman, 41, Manhasset, NY
October 24, 1959

Margaret M. Seeliger, 34, New York, NY
December 28, 1966

Anthony Segarra, 52, New York, NY
October 16, 1949

Carlos Segarra, 54, New York, NY
September 24, 1946

Jason Sekzer, 31, New York, NY
June 5, 1970

Matthew Carmen Sellitto, 23, New Vernon, NJ
September 30, 1977

Howard Selwyn, 47, Hewlett, NY
August 2, 1954

Larry John Senko, 34, Yardley, PA
February 20, 1967

Arturo Angelo Sereno, 29, New York, NY
December 6, 1971

Frankie Serrano, 23, Elizabeth, NJ
September 23, 1977

Alena Sesinova, 57, New York, NY
June 16, 1944

Adele Christine Sessa, 36, New York, NY
September 4, 1965

Sita Nermalla Sewnarine, 37, New York, NY
February 14, 1964

Karen Lynn Seymour, 40, Millington, NJ
November 6, 1960

Davis Grier Sezna, Jr., 22, New York, NY
December 22, 1978

Thomas Joseph Sgroi, 45, New York, NY
January 20, 1956

Jayesh Shantilal Shah, 38, Edgewater, NJ
April 17, 1963

Khalid M. Shahid, 25, Union, NJ
May 3, 1976

Mohammed Shajahan, 41, Spring Valley, NY
June 3, 1960

Gary Shamay, 23, New York, NY
February 6, 1978

Earl Richard Shanahan, 50, New York, NY
September 28, 1950

Neil G. Shastri, 25, New York, NY
August 17, 1976

Kathryn Anne Shatzoff, 37, New York, NY
June 9, 1964

Barbara A. Shaw, 57, Morris Township, NJ
July 17, 1944

Jeffrey James Shaw, 42, Levittown, NY
July 2, 1959

Robert J. Shay, Jr., 27, New York, NY
June 23, 1974

Daniel James Shea, 37, Pelham Manor, NY
February 26, 1964

Joseph Patrick Shea, 47, Pelham, NY
August 4, 1954

Linda June Sheehan, 40, New York, NY
December 16, 1960

Hagay Shefi, 34, Tenafly, NJ
October 24, 1966

John Anthony Sherry, 34, Rockville Centre, NY
September 20, 1966

Clarin Shellie Siegel-Schwartz, 51, New York, NY
November 14, 1949

Atsushi Shiratori, 36, New York, NY
April 11, 1965

Thomas John Shubert, 43, Tuckahoe, NY
February 4, 1958

Mark Shulman, 47, Old Bridge, NJ
March 27, 1954

See Wong Shum, 44, Westfield, NJ
December 24, 1956

Allan Shwartzstein, 37, Pleasantville, NY
March 31, 1964

Johanna Sigmund, 25, New York, NY
June 21, 1976

Dianne T. Signer, 32, New York, NY
March 23, 1969

Gregory Sikorsky, 34, Spring Valley, NY
October 5, 1966

Stephen Gerard Siller, 34, New York, NY
November 15, 1966

David Silver, 35, New Rochelle, NY
March 14, 1966

Craig A. Silverstein, 41, Wyckoff, NJ
August 10, 1960

Nasima H. Simjee, 38, New York, NY
December 27, 1962

Bruce Edward Simmons, 41, Ridgewood, NJ
August 13, 1960

Arthur Simon, 57, Thiells, NY
May 5, 1944

Kenneth Alan Simon, 34, Secaucus, NJ
July 12, 1967

Michael John Simon, 40, Harrington Park, NJ
July 27, 1961

Paul Joseph Simon, 54, New York, NY
March 31, 1947

Marianne Liquori Simone, 62, New York, NY
March 4, 1939

Barry Simowitz, 64, New York, NY
January 16, 1937

Jeff Lyal Simpson, 38, Woodbridge, VA
May 14, 1963

Khamladai Khami Singh, 25, New York, NY
April 21, 1976

Roshan Ramesh Singh, 21, New York, NY
August 6, 1980

Thomas E. Sinton III, 44, Croton-on-Hudson, NY
July 23, 1960

Peter A. Siracuse, 29, New York, NY
April 20, 1972

Muriel F. Siskopoulos, 60, New York, NY
April 4, 1941

Joseph Michael Sisolak, 35, New York, NY
June 3, 1966

John P. Skala, 31, Clifton, NJ
June 30, 1970

Francis Joseph Skidmore, Jr., 58, Mendham, NJ
June 4, 1943

Toyena Corliss Skinner, 27, Kingston, NJ
November 26, 1973

Paul A. Skrzypek, 37, New York, NY
July 11, 1964

Christopher Paul Slattery, 31, New York, NY
December 30, 1969

Vincent Robert Slavin, 41, New York, NY
January 31, 1960

Robert F. Sliwak, 42, Wantagh, NY
October 26, 1958

Paul Kenneth Sloan, 26, New York, NY
July 30, 1975

Stanley S. Smagala, Jr., 36, Holbrook, NY
April 6, 1965

Wendy L. Small, 26, New York, NY
July 16, 1975

Catherine T. Smith, 44, Manahwkin, NJ
November 22, 1956

Daniel Laurence Smith, 47, Northport, NY
October 27, 1953

George Eric Smith, 38, West Chester, PA
January 21, 1963

James Gregory Smith, 43, Garden City, NY
October 27, 1957

Jeffrey R. Smith, 36, New York, NY
April 19, 1965

Joyce Patricia Smith, 55, New York, NY
December 16, 1945

Karl T. Smith, Sr., 44, Little Silver, NJ
June 12, 1957

Kevin Joseph Smith, 47, Mastic, NY
August 20, 1954

Leon Smith, Jr., 48, New York, NY
July 14, 1953

Moira Ann Smith, 38, New York, NY
February 14, 1963

Rosemary A. Smith, 61, New York, NY
April 27, 1940

Bonnie Shihadeh Smithwick, 54, Quogue, NY
January 15, 1947

Rochelle Monique Snell, 24, Mount Vernon, NY
November 15, 1976

Leonard J. Snyder, Jr., 35, Cranford, NJ
July 30, 1967

Astrid Elizabeth Sohan, 32, Freehold, NJ
September 25, 1968

Sushil S. Solanki, 35, New York, NY
January 6, 1966

Rubén Solares, 51, New York, NY
May 7, 1950

Naomi Leah Solomon, 52, New York, NY
July 28, 1949

Daniel W. Song, 34, New York, NY
May 21, 1967

Michael Charles Sorresse, 34, Parsippany, NJ
October 17, 1966

Fabian Soto, 31, Harrison, NJ
May 13, 1970

Timothy Patrick Soulas, 35, Basking Ridge, NJ
August 11, 1966

Gregory Thomas Spagnoletti, 32, New York, NY
October 18, 1968

Donald F. Spampinato, Jr., 39, Manhasset, NY
September 15, 1961

Thomas Sparacio, 35, New York, NY
March 21, 1966

John Anthony Spataro, 32, Mineola, NY
March 16, 1969

Robert W. Spear, Jr., 30, Valley Cottage, NY
January 30, 1971

Maynard S. Spence, Jr., 42, Atlanta, GA
December 26, 1958

George Edward Spencer III, 50, West Norwalk, CT
September 5, 1951

Robert Andrew Spencer, 35, Red Bank, NJ
March 15, 1966

Mary Rubina Sperando, 39, New York, NY
September 29, 1961

Frank J. Spinelli, 44, Short Hills, NJ
October 10, 1956

William E. Spitz, 49, Oceanside, NY
April 9, 1952

Joseph Patrick Spor, 35, Yorktown Heights, NY
July 21, 1966

Klaus Johannes Sprockamp, 42, Muhltal, Germany
October 30, 1958

Saranya Srinuan, 23, New York, NY
August 17, 1978

Fitzroy St. Rose, 40, New York, NY
April 19, 1961

Michael F. Stabile, 50, New York, NY
January 11, 1951

Lawrence T. Stack, 58, Lake Ronkonkoma, NY
December 10, 1942

Capt. Timothy M. Stackpole, 42, New York, NY
January 18, 1959

Richard James Stadelberger, 55, Middletown, NJ
February 12, 1946

Eric Adam Stahlman, 43, Holmdel Township, NJ
June 13, 1958

Gregory M. Stajk, 46, Long Beach, NY
February 12, 1955

Corina Stan, 31, Middle Village, NY
March 6, 1970

Alexandru Liviu Stan, 34, New York, NY
September 8, 1967

Mary Domenica Stanley, 53, New York, NY
November 19, 1947

Anthony M. Starita, 35, Westfield, NJ
June 10, 1966

Jeffrey Stark, 30, New York, NY
April 5, 1971

Derek James Statkevicus, 30, Norwalk, CT
May 26, 1971

Craig William Staub, 30, Basking Ridge, NJ
September 22, 1970

William V. Steckman, 56, Hempstead, NY
December 24, 1944

Eric Thomas Steen, 32, New York, NY
December 14, 1968

William R. Steiner, 56, Solebury, PA
April 18, 1945

Alexander Robbins Steinman, 32, Hoboken, NJ
January 12, 1969

Andrew Stergiopoulos, 23, New York, NY
March 7, 1978

Andrew J. Stern, 41, Bellmore, NY
June 27, 1960

Martha Jane Stevens, 55, New York, NY
June 19, 1946

Michael James Stewart, 42, New York, NY
June 20, 1959

Richard H. Stewart, Jr., 35, New York, NY
August 14, 1966

Sanford M. Stoller, 54, New York, NY
August 5, 1947

Lonny Jay Stone, 43, Bellmore, NY
June 8, 1958

Jimmy Nevill Storey, 58, Katy, TX
March 6, 1943

Timothy Stout, 42, Dobbs Ferry, NY
August 19, 1959

Thomas Strada, 41, Chatham, NJ
July 1, 1960

James J. Straine, Jr., 36, Oceanport, NJ
February 5, 1965

Edward W. Straub, 48, Morris Township, NJ
April 26, 1953

George J. Strauch, Jr., 53, Avon-by-the-Sea, NJ
February 6, 1948

Edward Thomas Strauss, 44, Edison, NJ
August 28, 1957

Steven R. Strauss, 51, New York, NY
November 17, 1949

Steven F. Strobert, 33, Ridgewood, NJ
November 10, 1967

Walwyn Wellington Stuart, Jr., 28, Valley Stream, NY
February 13, 1973

Benjamin Suarez, 36, New York, NY
October 10, 1966

David Scott Suarez, 24, Princeton Junction, NJ
October 30, 1976

Ramón Suárez, 45, New York, NY
April 6, 1956

Yoichi Sugiyama, 34, Fort Lee, NJ
August 17, 1967

William Christopher Sugra, 30, New York, NY
August 6, 1971

Daniel Thomas Suhr, 37, Nesconset, NY
August 21, 1964

David Marc Sullins, 30, New York, NY
June 13, 1971

Lt. Christopher P. Sullivan, 38, North Massapequa, NY
July 28, 1962

Patrick Sullivan, 32, New York, NY
June 7, 1969

Thomas G. Sullivan, 38, Kearney, NJ
December 6, 1962

Hilario Soriano Sumaya, Jr., 42, New York, NY
September 19, 1958

James Joseph Suozzo, 47, Hauppauge, NY
June 18, 1954

Colleen M. Supinski, 27, New York, NY
August 24, 1974

Robert Sutcliffe, 39, Huntington, NY
October 16, 1961

Selina Sutter, 63, New York, NY
September 14, 1937

Claudia Suzette Sutton, 34, New York, NY
December 15, 1966

John Francis Swaine, 36, Larchmont, NY
October 27, 1964

Kristine M. Swearson, 34, New York, NY
September 4, 1967

Brian Edward Sweeney, 29, Merrick, NY
November 10, 1971

Kenneth J. Swensen, 40, Chatham, NJ
May 13, 1961

Thomas F. Swift, 30, Jersey City, NJ
December 2, 1970

Derek Ogilvie Sword, 29, New York, NY
November 30, 1971

Kevin Thomas Szocik, 27, Garden City, NY
August 19, 1974

Gina Sztejnberg, 52, Ridgewood, NJ
February 14, 1949

Norbert P. Szurkowski, 31, New York, NY
September 2, 1970

T

Harry Taback, 56, New York, NY
March 21, 1945

Joann C. Tabeek, 41, New York, NY
February 8, 1960

Norma C. Taddei, 64, New York, NY
August 13, 1937

Michael Taddonio, 39, Huntington, NY
April 2, 1962

Keiichiro Takahashi, 53, Port Washington, NY
April 8, 1948

Keiji Takahashi, 42, Tenafly, NJ
March 27, 1959

Phyllis Gail Talbot, 53, New York, NY
April 14, 1948

Robert R. Talhami, 40, Shrewsbury, NJ
May 17, 1961

Sean Patrick Tallon, 26, Yonkers, NY
September 27, 1971

Paul Talty, 40, Wantagh, NY
November 23, 1960

Maurita Tam, 22, New York, NY
February 18, 1979

Rachel Tamares, 30, New York, NY
November 19, 1970

Hector Rogan Tamayo, 51, New York, NY
January 15, 1950

Michael Andrew Tamuccio, 37, Pelham Manor, NY
April 14, 1964

Kenichiro Tanaka, 52, Rye Brook, NY
October 25, 1948

Rhondelle Cherie Tankard, 31, Devonshire, Bermuda
January 3, 1970

Michael Anthony Tanner, 44, Secaucus, NJ
March 22, 1957

Dennis Gerard Taormina, Jr., 36, Montville, NJ
February 17, 1965

Kenneth Joseph Tarantino, 39, Bayonne, NJ
December 25, 1961

Allan Tarasiewicz, 45, New York, NY
January 24, 1956

Ronald Tartaro, 39, Bridgewater, NJ
March 12, 1963

Darryl Anthony Taylor, 52, New York, NY
June 1, 1949

Donnie Brooks Taylor, 40, New York, NY
June 15, 1961

Lorisa Ceylon Taylor, 31, New York, NY
December 17, 1969

Michael Morgan Taylor, 42, New York, NY
August 26, 1959

Paul A. Tegtmeier, 41, Hyde Park, NY
March 24, 1960

Yeshavant Moreshwar Tembe, 59, Piscataway, NJ
February 2, 1942

Anthony Tempesta, 38, Elizabeth, NJ
June 13, 1963

Dorothy Pearl Temple, 52, New York, NY
August 8, 1949

Stanley L. Temple, 77, New York, NY
May 17, 1924

David Gustaf Peter Tengelin, 25, New York, NY
March 18, 1976

Brian John Terrenzi, 29, Hicksville, NY
September 21, 1972

Lisa Marie Terry, 42, Oakland Township, MI
January 31, 1959

Goumatie T. Thackurdeen, 35, New York, NY
May 23, 1966

Harshad Sham Thatte, 30, Norcross, GA
December 16, 1970

Thomas F. Theurkauf, Jr., 44, Stamford, CT
February 16, 1957

Lesley Anne Thomas, 40, Hoboken, NJ
May 30, 1960

Brian Thomas Thompson, 49, Dix Hills, NY
February 24, 1952

Clive Ian Thompson, 43, Summit, NJ
July 5, 1958

Glenn Thompson, 44, New York, NY
June 4, 1957

Nigel Bruce Thompson, 33, New York, NY
February 25, 1968

Perry Anthony Thompson, 36, Mount Laurel, NJ
May 10, 1965

Vanavah Alexi Thompson, 26, New York, NY
July 15, 1975

Capt. William Harry Thompson, 51, New York, NY
July 20, 1950

Eric Raymond Thorpe, 35, New York, NY
April 17, 1966

Nichola Angela Thorpe, 22, New York, NY
October 10, 1978

Sal Edward Tieri, Jr., 40, Shrewsbury, NJ
March 2, 1961

John Patrick Tierney, 27, New York, NY
August 2, 1974

Mary Ellen Tiesi, 38, Jersey City, NJ
January 1, 1963

William Randolph Tieste, 54, Basking Ridge, NJ
December 1, 1946

Kenneth Tietjen, 31, Matawan, NJ
July 4, 1970

Stephen Edward Tighe, 41, Rockville Centre, NY
October 1, 1959

Scott Charles Timmes, 28, Ridgewood, NY
June 26, 1973

Michael E. Tinley, 56, Dallas, TX
January 12, 1945

Jennifer M. Tino, 29, Livingston, NJ
April 29, 1972

Robert Frank Tipaldi, 25, New York, NY
May 6, 1976

John James Tipping II, 33, Hauppauge, NY
January 4, 1968

David Tirado, 26, New York, NY
February 14, 1975

Hector Luis Tirado, Jr., 30, New York, NY
July 7, 1971

Michelle Lee Titolo, 34, Copiague, NY
May 25, 1967

John J. Tobin, 47, Kenilworth, NJ
February 18, 1954

Richard J. Todisco, 61, Wyckoff, NJ
July 1, 1940

Vladimir Tomasevic, 36, Etobicoke, Ontario, Canada
January 25, 1965

Stephen Kevin Tompsett, 39, Garden City, NY
January 27, 1962

Thomas Tong, 31, New York, NY
November 6, 1969

Luis Eduardo Torres, 31, New York, NY
December 31, 1969

Amy Elizabeth Toyen, 24, Newton, MA
June 20, 1977

Christopher Michael Traina, 25, Bricktown, NJ
June 28, 1976

Daniel Patrick Trant, 40, Northport, NY
May 15, 1961

Abdoul Karim Traore, 41, New York, NY
January 14, 1961

Glenn J. Travers, Sr., 53, Tenafly, NJ
January 13, 1948

Walter Philip Travers, 44, Upper Saddle River, NJ
May 22, 1957

Felicia Yvette Traylor-Bass, 38, New York, NY
July 26, 1963

Lisa L. Trerotola, 38, Hazlet, NJ
September 30, 1964

Karamo Baba Trerra, 40, New York, NY
August 2, 1961

Michael Angel Trinidad, 33, New York, NY
March 26, 1968

Francis Joseph Trombino, 68, Clifton, NJ
January 30, 1933

Gregory James Trost, 26, New York, NY
March 17, 1975

William P. Tselepis, Jr., 33, New Providence, NJ
February 17, 1968

Zhanetta Valentinovna Tsoy, 32, Jersey City, NJ
October 5, 1968

Michael Patrick Tucker, 40, Rumson, NJ
November 22, 1961

Lance Richard Tumulty, 32, Bridgewater, NJ
March 31, 1969

Ching Ping Tung, 44, New York, NY
July 3, 1957

Simon James Turner, 39, London, England
July 17, 1962

Donald Joseph Tuzio, 51, Goshen, NY
February 11, 1950

Robert T. Twomey, 48, New York, NY
September 26, 1952

Jennifer Lynn Tzemis, 26, New York, NY
October 30, 1974

U

John G. Ueltzhoeffer, 36, Roselle Park, NJ
February 13, 1965

Tyler Victor Ugolyn, 23, New York, NY
August 7, 1978

Michael A. Uliano, 42, Aberdeen, NJ
September 2, 1959

Jonathan J. Uman, 33, Westport, CT
February 4, 1968

Anil Shivhari Umarkar, 34, Hackensack, NJ
July 30, 1967

Allen V. Upton, 44, New York, NY
June 6, 1957

Diane Maria Urban, 50, Malverne, NY
May 1, 1951

V

John Damien Vaccacio, 30, New York, NY
April 15, 1971

William Valcarcel, 54, New York, NY
November 14, 1946

Mayra Valdes Rodríguez, 39, New York, NY
February 4, 1962

Felix Antonio Vale, 29, New York, NY
July 23, 1972

Ivan Vale, 27, New York, NY
May 9, 1974

Benito Valentin, 33, New York, NY
January 20, 1968

Santos Valentin, 39, New York, NY
October 22, 1961

Carlton Francis Valvo, 38, New York, NY
July 25, 1963

R. Bruce Van Hine, 48, Greenwood Lake, NY
July 25, 1953

Daniel M. Van Laere, 46, Glen Rock, NJ
January 13, 1955

Edward Raymond Vanacore, 29, Jersey City, NJ
April 15, 1972

Jon Charles Vandevander, 44, Ridgewood, NJ
August 18, 1957

Frederick T. Varacchi, 35, Greenwich, CT
December 21, 1965

Gopalakrishnan Varadhan, 32, New York, NY
January 3, 1969

David Vargas, 46, New York, NY
December 30, 1954

Scott C. Vasel, 32, Park Ridge, NJ
June 3, 1969

Azael Ismael Vasquez, 21, New York, NY
July 12, 1980

Santos Vasquez, 55, New York, NY
May 11, 1946

Arcangel Vazquez, 47, New York, NY
June 29, 1954

Peter Vega, 36, New York, NY
June 15, 1965

Sankara Sastry Velamuri, 63, Avenel, NJ
September 24, 1937

Jorge Velazquez, 47, Passaic, NJ
April 23, 1954

Lawrence G. Veling, 44, New York, NY
October 29, 1956

Anthony Mark Ventura, 41, Middletown, NJ
June 12, 1960

David Vera, 41, New York, NY
August 4, 1960

Loretta Ann Vero, 51, Nanuet, NY
August 4, 1950

Christopher James Vialonga, 30, Demarest, NJ
February 2, 1971

Matthew Gilbert Vianna, 23, Manhasset, NY
August 14, 1978

Robert Anthony Vicario, 40, Weehawken, NJ
October 16, 1960

Celeste Torres Victoria, 41, New York, NY
February 21, 1960

Joanna Vidal, 26, Yonkers, NY
November 3, 1974

John T. Vigiano, 36, West Islip, NY
December 8, 1964

Joseph Vincent Vigiano, 34, Medford, NY
April 5, 1967

Frank J. Vignola, 44, Merrick, NY
July 6, 1957

Joseph Barry Vilardo, 44, Stanhope, NJ
April 10, 1959

Sergio Gabriel Villanueva, 33, New York, NY
July 4, 1968

Chantal Vincelli, 38, New York, NY
March 31, 1963

Melissa Renée Vincent, 28, Hoboken, NJ
October 24, 1972

Francine Ann Virgilio, 48, New York, NY
June 7, 1953

Lawrence Virgilio, 38, New York, NY
December 31, 1962

Joseph Gerard Visciano, 22, New York, NY
February 25, 1979

Joshua S. Vitale, 28, Great Neck, NY
January 30, 1973

Maria Percoco Vola, 37, New York, NY
March 30, 1963

Lynette D. Vosges, 48, New York, NY
June 4, 1953

Garo H. Voskerijian, 43, Valley Stream, NY
July 26, 1958

Alfred Anton Vukosa, 37, New York, NY
July 16, 1964

W

Gregory Kamal Bruno Wachtler, 25, Ramsey, NJ
February 7, 1976

Gabriela Silvina Waisman, 33, New York, NY
May 20, 1968

Wendy Alice Rosario Wakeford, 40, Freehold, NJ
August 6, 1961

Courtney Wainsworth Walcott, 37, New York, NY
March 23, 1964

Victor Wald, 49, New York, NY
November 23, 1951

Benjamin James Walker, 41, Suffern, NY
August 2, 1960

Glen Wall, 38, Rumson, NJ
October 13, 1962

Mitchel Scott Wallace, 34, Mineola, NY
March 11, 1967

Peter Guyder Wallace, 66, Lincoln Park, NJ
January 22, 1935

Lt. Robert Francis Wallace, 43, New York, NY
April 3, 1958

Roy Michael Wallace, 42, Wyckoff, NJ
December 24, 1958

Jeanmarie Wallendorf, 23, New York, NY
August 7, 1978

Matthew Blake Wallens, 31, New York, NY
April 16, 1970

John Wallice, 43, Huntington, NY
September 29, 1957

Barbara P. Walsh, 59, New York, NY
May 3, 1942

Jim Walsh, 37, Scotch Plains, NJ
February 19, 1964

Jeffrey Patrick Walz, 37, Tuckahoe, NY
March 29, 1964

Weibin Wang, 41, Orangeburg, NY
June 14, 1960

Lt. Michael Warchola, 51, Middle Village, NY
February 20, 1950

Stephen Gordon Ward, 33, Gorham, ME
April 9, 1968

James A. Waring, 49, New York, NY
August 2, 1952

Brian G. Warner, 32, Morganville, NJ
November 9, 1968

Derrick Christopher Washington, 33, Calverton, NY
March 8, 1968

Charles Waters, 44, New York, NY
August 26, 1957

James Thomas Waters, 39, New York, NY
September 4, 1962

Capt. Patrick J. Waters, 44, New York, NY
December 6, 1956

Kenneth Thomas Watson, 39, Smithtown, NY
January 8, 1962

Michael Henry Waye, 38, Morganville, NJ
February 19, 1963

Walter Edward Weaver, 30, Centereach, NY
July 22, 1971

Todd Christopher Weaver, 30, New York, NY
December 31, 1970

Nathaniel Webb, 56, Jersey City, NJ
December 2, 1944

Dinah Webster, 50, Port Washington, NY
December 16, 1950

Joanne Flora Weil, 39, New York, NY
April 25, 1962

Michael T. Weinberg, 34, New York, NY
January 19, 1967

Steven Weinberg, 41, New City, NY
December 7, 1959

Scott Jeffrey Weingard, 29, New York, NY
September 23, 1971

Steven George Weinstein, 50, New York, NY
April 13, 1951

Simon Weiser, 65, New York, NY
June 30, 1936

David M. Weiss, 41, Maybrook, NY
July 21, 1960

David Thomas Weiss, 50, New York, NY
April 6, 1951

Vincent Michael Wells, 22, Redbridge, England
September 17, 1978

Timothy Matthew Welty, 34, Yonkers, NY
February 27, 1967

Christian Hans Rudolf Wemmers, 43, San Francisco, CA
October 12, 1958

Ssu-Hui (Vanessa) Wen, 23, New York, NY
November 1, 1977

Oleh D. Wengerchuk, 56, Centerport, NY
October 4, 1944

Peter M. West, 54, Pottersville, NJ
November 5, 1946

Whitfield West, 41, New York, NY
February 24, 1960

Meredith Lynn Whalen, 23, Hoboken, NJ
August 9, 1978

Eugene Michael Whelan, 31, Rockaway Beach, NY
November 23, 1969

Adam S. White, 26, New York, NY
September 26, 1974

John Sylvester White, 48, New York, NY
May 25, 1953

Edward James White III, 30, New York, NY
January 25, 1971

James Patrick White, 34, Hoboken, NJ
July 22, 1967

Kenneth Wilburn White, 50, New York, NY
September 24, 1950

Leonard Anthony White, 57, New York, NY
February 13, 1944

Malissa Y. White, 37, New York, NY
June 19, 1964

Wayne White, 38, New York, NY
November 5, 1963

Leanne Marie Whiteside, 31, New York, NY
April 30, 1970

Mark P. Whitford, 31, Salisbury Mills, NY
April 5, 1970

Michael T. Wholey, 34, Westwood, NJ
September 26, 1966

Mary Lenz Wieman, 43, Rockville Centre, NY
June 14, 1958

Jeffrey David Wiener, 33, New York, NY
February 14, 1968

William J. Wik, 44, Crestwood, NY
May 13, 1957

Alison Marie Wildman, 30, New York, NY
April 10, 1971

Lt. Glenn E. Wilkinson, 46, Bayport, NY
April 19, 1955

John Charles Willett, 29, Jersey City, NJ
November 29, 1971

Brian Patrick Williams, 29, New York, NY
May 8, 1972

Crossley Richard Williams, 28, Uniondale, NY
February 19, 1973

David J. Williams, 34, New York, NY
June 4, 1967

Debbie Lynn Williams, 35, Hoboken, NJ
April 22, 1966

Kevin Michael Williams, 24, New York, NY
August 23, 1977

Louie Anthony Williams, 44, New York, NY
May 19, 1957

Louis Calvin Williams III, 53, Mandeville, LA
August 17, 1948

Lt. John P. Williamson, 46, Warwick, NY
November 17, 1954

Donna Ann Wilson, 48, Williston Park, NY
March 29, 1953

William Eben Wilson, 58, New York, NY
April 18, 1943

David Harold Winton, 29, New York, NY
January 5, 1972

Glenn J. Winuk, 40, New York, NY
May 5, 1961

Thomas Francis Wise, 43, New York, NY
September 26, 1957

Alan L. Wisniewski, 47, Howell, NJ
June 5, 1954

Frank Paul Wisniewski, 54, Basking Ridge, NJ
February 10, 1947

David Wiswall, 54, North Massapequa, NY
February 27, 1947

Sigrid Charlotte Wiswe, 41, New York, NY
October 29, 1959

Michael R. Wittenstein, 34, Hoboken, NJ
February 1, 1967

Christopher W. Wodenshek, 35, Ridgewood, NJ
September 22, 1965

Martin Phillips Wohlforth, 47, Greenwich, CT
October 22, 1953

Katherine Susan Wolf, 40, New York, NY
June 15, 1961

Jennifer Y. Wong, 26, New York, NY
May 16, 1975

Jenny Seu Kueng Low Wong, 25, New York, NY
August 27, 1976

Yin Ping (Steven) Wong, 34, New York, NY
April 1, 1967

Yuk Ping Wong, 47, New York, NY
April 26, 1954

Brent James Woodall, 31, Oradell, NJ
July 20, 1970

James John Woods, 26, New York, NY
February 26, 1975

Patrick J. Woods, 36, New York, NY
July 19, 1965

Richard Herron Woodwell, 44, Ho-Ho-Kus, N.J.
June 18, 1957

Capt. David Terence Wooley, 54, Nanuet, NY
May 1, 1947

John Bentley Works, 36, Darien, CT
October 24, 1964

Martin Michael Wortley, 29, Park Ridge, NJ
November 21, 1971

Rodney James Wotton, 36, Middletown, NJ
January 4, 1965

William Wren, 61, Lynbrook, NY
August 12, 1940

John W. Wright, 33, Rockville Centre, NY
December 14, 1967

Neil Robin Wright, 30, Asbury, NJ
May 28, 1971

Sandra Lee Wright, 57, Langhorne, PA
August 7, 1944

X-Y

Jupiter Yambem, 41, Beacon, NY
November 4, 1959

Suresh Yanamadala, 33, Plainsboro, NJ
August 30, 1968

Matthew David Yarnell, 26, Jersey City, NJ
July 31, 1975

Myrna Yaskulka, 59, New York, NY
November 11, 1941

Shakila Yasmin, 26, New York, NY
August 20, 1975

Olabisi Shadie Layeni Yee, 38, New York, NY
January 2, 1963

Edward P. York, 45, Wilton, CT
May 6, 1956

Kevin Patrick York, 41, Princeton, NJ
September 6, 1960

Raymond York, 45, Valley Stream, NY
March 21, 1956

Suzanne Youmans, 60, New York, NY
December 27, 1940

Barrington L. Young, 35, New York, NY
May 17, 1966

Jacqueline (Jakki) Young, 37, New York, NY
March 10, 1954

Elkin Yuen, 32, New York, NY
October 17, 1968

Z

Joseph Zaccoli, 39, Valley Stream, NY
January 9, 1962

Adel Agayby Zakhary, 50, North Arlington, NJ
January 1, 1951

Arkady Zaltsman, 45, New York, NY
December 1, 1955

Edwin J. Zambrana, 24, New York, NY
July 5, 1977

Robert Alan Zampieri, 30, Saddle River, NJ
October 8, 1970

Mark Zangrilli, 36, Pompton Plains, NJ
May 3, 1965

Ira Zaslow, 55, North Woodmere, NY
February 28, 1946

Kenneth Albert Zelman, 37, Succasunna, NJ
October 12, 1964

Abraham J. Zelmanowitz, 55, New York, NY
December 30, 1945

Martin Morales Zempoaltecatl, 22, New York, NY
February 23, 1979

Zhe (Zack) Zeng, 28, New York, NY
September 30, 1972

Marc Scott Zeplin, 33, Harrison, NY
February 12, 1968

Jie Yao Justin Zhao, 27, New York, NY
May 21, 1974

Ivelin Ziminski, 40, Tarrytown, NY
July 2, 1960

Michael Joseph Zinzi, 37, Newfoundland, NJ
September 2, 1964

Charles A. Zion, 54, Greenwich, CT
March 1, 1947

Julie Lynne Zipper, 44, Paramus, NJ
November 18, 1956

Salvatore J. Zisa, 45, Hawthorne, NJ
January 5, 1956

Prokopios Paul Zois, 46, Lynbrook, NY
April 25, 1955

Joseph J. Zuccala, 54, Croton-on-Hudson, NY
November 13, 1946

Andrew Steven Zucker, 27, New York, NY
January 5, 1974

Igor Zukelman, 29, New York, NY
June 25, 1972

The Others

Hijackers

The nineteen young men who carried out these terrorist attacks were misguided.
Yet each one had a mother, a father, and family. None was beyond redemption or forgiveness.
Out of respect for the victims who died that day, however, the hijackers are listed here
in order of their birthdays, not by name.

February 2, 1981

March 19, 1977

May 9, 1978

May 11, 1975

May 16, 1975

May 28, 1979

June 18, 1977

June 28, 1976

July 2, 1979

July 31, 1973

August 9, 1976

August 13, 1972

August 17, 1977

August 17, 1979

September 1, 1968

October 11, 1980

November 18, 1980

November 21, 1979

December 20, 1978

First Responders

Following are the names of the first responders honored at the 9/11 Memorial, listed alphabetically by last name.

A

Brian G. Ahearn
Eric Allen
Richard Dennis Allen
James M. Amato
Joseph Amatuccio
Christopher Charles Amoroso
Calixto Anaya, Jr.
Joseph Angelini, Sr.
Joseph John Angelini, Jr.
Faustino Apostol, Jr.
David Gregory Arce
Louis Arena
Carl Francis Asaro
Gregg A. Atlas
Gerald Thomas Atwood

B

Gerard Baptiste
Gerard A. Barbara
James William Barbella
Matthew Barnes
Arthur Thaddeus Barry
Maurice Vincent Barry
Steven Joseph Bates
Carl John Bedigian
Stephen Elliot Belson
John P. Bergin
Paul Michael Beyer
Peter Alexander Bielfeld
Brian Eugene Bilcher
Carl Vincent Bini
Christopher Joseph Blackwell
Michael L. Bocchino
Lawrence Francis Boisseau
Frank J. Bonomo
Gary R. Box
Michael Boyle
Kevin Hugh Bracken

Michael E. Brennan
Peter Brennan
Daniel J. Brethel
Patrick John Brown
Andrew Brunn
Vincent Edward Brunton
Ronald Bucca
Greg J. Buck
William Francis Burke, Jr.
Donald J. Burns
John Patrick Burnside
Thomas M. Butler
Patrick Dennis Byrne

C

George C. Cain
Salvatore B. Calabro
Edward Calderon
Francis Joseph Callahan
Liam Callahan
Michael F. Cammarata
Brian Cannizzaro
Dennis M. Carey, Sr.
Michael Scott Carlo
Michael T. Carroll
Peter J. Carroll
Thomas Anthony Casoria
Michael Joseph Cawley
Vernon Paul Cherry
Nicholas Paul Chiofalo
John G. Chipura
Robert D. Cirri Sr.
Michael J. Clarke
Steven Coakley
Tarel Coleman
John Michael Collins
Robert Joseph Cordice
Ruben D. Correa
James J. Corrigan, Ret.
John G. Coughlin

James Raymond Coyle
Robert James Crawford
John A. Crisci
Dennis A. Cross
Thomas Patrick Cullen III
Robert Curatolo
Michael Sean Curtin
John D'Allara
Edward A. D'Atri
Michael D. D'Auria
Carlos S. da Costa

D

Vincent G. Danz
Scott Matthew Davidson
Clinton Davis, Sr.
Edward James Day
Thomas Patrick DeAngelis
Manuel Del Valle, Jr.
Francis Albert De Martini
Martin N. DeMeo
David Paul DeRubbio
Andrew J. Desperito
Dennis Lawrence Devlin
Gerard P. Dewan
George DiPasquale
Jerome Mark Patrick Dominguez
Kevin W. Donnelly
Kevin Christopher Dowdell
Raymond Matthew Downey, Sr.
Stephen Patrick Driscoll
Gerard J. Duffy

E

Martin J. Egan, Jr.
Michael J. Elferis

Mark Joseph Ellis
Francis Esposito
Michael A. Esposito
Robert Edward Evans

F

Keith George Fairben
John Joseph Fanning
Thomas James Farino
Terrence Patrick Farrell
Joseph D. Farrelly
Robert Fazio, Jr.
William M. Feehan
Lee S. Fehling
Alan D. Feinberg
Michael C. Fiore
John R. Fischer
Richard P. Fitzsimons
Andre G. Fletcher
John Joseph Florio
Michael N. Fodor
Thomas J. Foley
David J. Fontana
Donald A. Foreman
Robert Joseph Foti
Clyde Frazier, Jr.
Andrew Fredericks
Peter L. Freund
Gregg J. Froehner

G

Thomas Gambino, Jr.
Peter James Ganci, Jr.
Charles William Garbarini
Thomas A. Gardner
Matthew David Garvey
Bruce Gary
Gary Paul Geidel
Edward F. Geraghty
Denis P. Germain

Vincent Francis Giammona
James Andrew Giberson
Ronnie E. Gies
Paul John Gill
Rodney C. Gillis
John F. Ginley
Jeffrey John Giordano
John Giordano
Keith Alexander Glascoe
Thomas Edward Gorman
James Michael Gray
Kenneth George Grouzalis
Joseph Grzelak
José A. Guadalupe
Geoffrey E. Guja
Joseph P. Gullickson

H

David Halderman
Vincent Gerard Halloran
Robert W. Hamilton
Sean S. Hanley
Thomas Paul Hannafin
Dana Rey Hannon
Daniel Edward Harlin
Harvey L. Harrell
Stephen G. Harrell
Thomas Theodore Haskell, Jr.
Timothy Shawn Haskell
Leonard W. Hatton, Jr.
Terence S. Hatton
Michael Helmut Haub
Philip T. Hayes, Ret.
Michael K. Healey
John F. Heffernan
Ronnie Lee Henderson
Joseph Patrick Henry
William L. Henry, Jr.
Thomas J. Hetzel
Brian Christopher Hickey
Timothy Brian Higgins
Jonathan R. Hohmann
Thomas P. Holohan
Uhuru G. Houston
George Gerard Howard
Stephen Huczko, Jr.

Joseph Gerard Hunter
Walter G. Hynes

I

Jonathan Lee Ielpi
Frederick J. Ill Jr.
Anthony P. Infante, Jr.

J

William R. Johnston
Andrew Brian Jordan, Sr.
Karl Henry Joseph
Anthony Jovic
Angel L. Juarbe, Jr.
Mychal F. Judge
Paul William Jurgens
Thomas Edward Jurgens

K

Vincent D. Kane
Douglas Gene Karpiloff
Charles L. Kasper
Robert Michael Kaulfers
Paul Hanlon Keating
Richard John Kelly, Jr.
Thomas Richard Kelly
Thomas W. Kelly
Thomas J. Kennedy
Ronald T. Kerwin
Michael Vernon Kiefer
Robert King, Jr.
Ronald Philip Kloepfer
Scott Michael Kopytko
William Edward Krukowski
Kenneth Bruce Kumpel
Thomas Joseph Kuveikis

L

David James LaForge
William David Lake
Robert T. Lane
Peter J. Langone
Thomas Michael Langone
Scott Larsen
Paul Laszczynski
James Patrick Leahy
Joseph Gerard Leavey
Neil J. Leavy

David Prudencio Lemagne
John Joseph Lennon, Jr.
John Dennis Levi
Daniel F. Libretti
Carlos R. Lillo
Robert Thomas Linnane
Joseph Lovero
James Francis Lynch
Michael Francis Lynch (FDNY Engine 40)
Michael Francis Lynch (FDNY Ladder 4)
Robert Henry Lynch Jr.
Michael J. Lyons
Patrick John Lyons

M

Joseph Maffeo
William J. Mahoney
Joseph E. Maloney
Joseph Ross Marchbanks, Jr.
Charles Joseph Margiotta
Kenneth Joseph Marino
John Daniel Marshall
Peter C. Martin
Paul Richard Martini
Joseph A. Mascali
Keithroy Marcellus Maynard
Robert J. Mayo
Kathy N. Mazza
Brian Gerard McAleese
John Kevin McAvoy
Thomas Joseph McCann
Brian Grady McDonnell
William E. McGinn
William J. McGovern
Dennis P. McHugh
Donald James McIntyre
Robert D. McMahon
Walter Arthur McNeil
Robert William McPadden
Terence A. McShane
Timothy Patrick McSweeney
Martin E. McWilliams
Raymond Meisenheimer
Charles R. Mendez

Steve John Mercado
Yamel Josefina Merino
Craig J. Miller
Douglas C. Miller
Henry Alfred Miller, Jr.
Charles M. Mills, Jr.
Robert J. Minara
Thomas Mingione
Paul Thomas Mitchell
Louis Joseph Modafferi
Dennis Mojica
Manuel D. Mojica, Jr.
Carl Molinaro
Michael G. Montesi
Thomas Carlo Moody
John Michael Moran
Vincent S. Morello
Richard J. Morgan
Ferdinand V. Morrone
Christopher Michael Mozzillo
Richard T. Muldowney, Jr.
Michael D. Mullan
Dennis Michael Mulligan
Raymond E. Murphy

N

Robert B. Nagel
John Philip Napolitano
Joseph M. Navas
Pete Negron
James A. Nelson
Peter Allen Nelson
Gerard Terence Nevins
Alfonse Joseph Niedermeyer

O

Dennis Patrick O'Berg
Daniel O'Callaghan
Douglas E. Oelschlager
Joseph J. Ogren
Thomas G. O'Hagan
Samuel Oitice
Patrick J. O'Keefe
William O'Keefe
Eric Taube Olsen
Jeffrey James Olsen
Steven John Olson

Kevin M. O'Rourke
David Ortiz
Michael John Otten

P

Jeffrey Matthew Palazzo
Orio Joseph Palmer
Frank Anthony Palombo
Paul J. Pansini
John M. Paolillo
Salvatore T. Papasso
James Nicholas Pappageorge
James Wendell Parham
Robert Parro
Richard Allen Pearlman
Durrell V. Pearsall, Jr.
Glenn C. Perry, Sr.
John William Perry
Philip Scott Petti
Glen Kerrin Pettit
Dominick A. Pezzulo
Kevin J. Pfeifer
Kenneth John Phelan, Sr.
Christopher J. Pickford
Shawn Edward Powell
Vincent A. Princiotta
Kevin M. Prior
Richard A. Prunty

Q

Lincoln Quappé
Michael T. Quilty
Ricardo J. Quinn

R

Leonard J. Ragaglia
Eugene J. Raggio
Michael Paul Ragusa
Edward J. Rall
Adam David Rand
Donald J. Regan
Robert M. Regan
Christian Michael Otto Regenhard
Kevin O. Reilly
Bruce Albert Reynolds
Francis Saverio Riccardelli
Vernon Allan Richard
Claude Daniel Richards
Jimmy Riches
Joseph R. Rivelli, Jr.
Michael E. Roberts
Michael Edward Roberts
Antonio José Rodrigues
Anthony Rodriguez
Richard Rodriguez
Matthew Rogan
Keith Michael Roma
James A. Romito
Nicholas P. Rossomando
Timothy Alan Roy, Sr.
Paul G. Ruback
Stephen P. Russell
Michael Thomas Russo, Sr.
Matthew L. Ryan

S

Thomas E. Sabella
Christopher A. Santora
John August Santore
Mario L. Santoro
Gregory Thomas Saucedo
Dennis Scauso
John Albert Schardt
Fred C. Scheffold, Jr.
Thomas G. Schoales
Gerard Patrick Schrang
Mark Schwartz
Gregory Sikorsky
Stephen Gerard Siller
Jeff Lyal Simpson
John P. Skala
Stanley S. Smagala, Jr.
Kevin Joseph Smith
Leon Smith, Jr.
Moira Ann Smith
Robert W. Spear, Jr.
Joseph Patrick Spor, Jr.
Lawrence T. Stack
Timothy M. Stackpole
Gregory Stajk
Jeffrey Stark
Edward Thomas Strauss
Walwyn Wellington Stuart, Jr.
Benjamin Suarez
Ramon Suarez
Daniel Thomas Suhr
David Marc Sullins
Christopher P. Sullivan
Brian Edward Sweeney

T

Sean Patrick Tallon
Paul Talty
Allan Tarasiewicz
Paul A. Tegtmeier
William H. Thompson
John Patrick Tierney
Kenneth Tietjen
John James Tipping II
Hector Luis Tirado, Jr.

U-V

Santos Valentin, Jr.
R. Bruce Van Hine
Peter Vega Lawrence G. Veling
John T. Vigiano II
Joseph Vincent Vigiano
Sergio Gabriel Villanueva
Lawrence Virgilio

W

Mitchel Scott Wallace
Robert Francis Wallace
Jeffrey P. Walz
Michael Warchola
Patrick J. Waters
Kenneth Thomas Watson
Walter Edward Weaver
Nathaniel Webb
Michael T. Weinberg
David M. Weiss
Timothy Matthew Welty
Eugene Michael Whelan
Edward James White III
Mark P. Whitford
Michael T. Wholey
Glenn E. Wilkinson
John P. Williamson
Glenn J. Winuk
David Terence Wooley
William Wren, Ret.

X-Y-Z

Raymond R. York

The Absent

The September 11 Memorial is a living tribute that continues to grow and evolve.

Its incomplete nature is evident in a single fact: not everyone who died at Ground Zero on September 11, 2001, is honored at the September 11 Memorial. Several undocumented workers employed illegally by the Windows on the World restaurant, as well as at least one bike messenger, are believed to have died when the towers collapsed. Alicia Acevedo Carranza, Víctor Antonio Martínez Pastrana, and Juan Romero Orozco, employed by Windows on the World, for example, are among those believed killed on September 11, 2001. Their names are absent from the Memorial.

Islam at the World Trade Center

The original World Trade Center was open to everyone. It welcomed all of humanity.

The number of Muslims who worked or conducted business in the Twin Towers was large enough to warrant an Islamic prayer room on the seventeenth floor of the South Tower. This place of worship was equipped with a washroom for the ritual ablution, known as wudu, for cleansing one's face, hands, and feet before intoning the salat prayer facing toward Mecca.

The rebuilt World Trade Center has no such accommodations.

Support

Donating to the September 11 Memorial and Museum

Royalties from the sale of this book are being donated to the September 11 Memorial and Museum.

Readers may send their donations to:

National September 11 Memorial and Museum at the World Trade Center Foundation, Inc.
200 Liberty Street, 16th Floor
New York, NY 10281

Editor's Notes

Astrological queries can be sent to 911.Astrology@gmail.com.

The six individuals killed during the first terrorist attack on the World Trade Center on February 26, 1993, are not included in this astrological tribute. John DiGiovanni, Robert Kirkpatrick, Stephen A. Knapp, Bill Macko, Wilfredo Mercado, and Monica Rodrigues Smith are, however, honored at the September 11 Memorial and Museum.

www.ingramcontent.com/pod-product-compliance
Lightning Source LLC
LaVergne TN
LVHW061345060426
835512LV00012B/2569